D1524463

you make the difference

**THE HANDBOOK FOR CADETTE
AND SENIOR GIRL SCOUTS**

Girl Scouts of the U.S.A.
830 Third Avenue
New York, N.Y. 10022

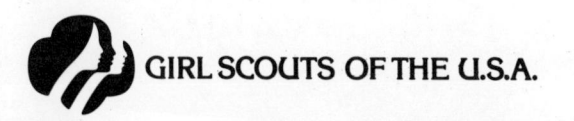 GIRL SCOUTS OF THE U.S.A.

Mrs. Orville L. Freeman, *President*
Mrs. Frances R. Hesselbein, *National Executive Director*

Inquiries related to *You Make the Difference: The Handbook for Cadette and Senior Girl Scouts* should be addressed to the Program Department, Girl Scouts of the U.S.A., 830 Third Avenue, New York, N.Y. 10022.

About the Cover: *Landscape #2* is the artist's title for this handsome silk-screen print. Seventeen-year-old Alex Tsui of Lexington, Mass., created it over a nine-week period, using tracing paper and photographic stencils to achieve the desired effect. *Landscape #2* won the gold medal for printmaking in *Scholastic Magazine*'s 1979 National Art and Photography Exhibition.

Special appreciation is extended to Scholastic Magazines, Inc. for use of award winning artwork and photography from their annual National Art and Photography Exhibitions.

You Make the Difference Contents

"As we learn responsibility and leadership, we learn to respect one another. As we grow in knowledge and understanding of ourselves, we grow, too, in knowledge and understanding of others. These bonds of respect and understanding are what develop our friendships and keep them strong.

"Our organization, as it responds to the changing ideas and values of our society, can present us with an opportunity for growth and leadership, which, in turn, can present our society with capable and caring leaders."

Patricia Kaiser, 17
Michigan Capitol Girl Scout Council
(Michigan)

"In ... Girl Scouting ... I have learned to communicate with the deaf, ... to plan and carry out ... camping trips, to raise money, to help others. ... With this type experience, it makes it easier for me to get a job. ..."

Lynne Pack, 17
Girl Scout Council of Greater Tidewater
(Virginia)

"More than anything, it's (Girl Scouting) brought me in touch with myself."

Jackie Sells, 14
Tribal Trails Girl Scout Council, Inc.
(Indiana)

"Soon our generation will be in charge of our country and the more we know about countries and their people, the better we are able to live together in peace and friendship."

Kalee Talritie, 14
Girl Scout Council of Buffalo and Erie County, Inc.
(New York)

"I feel very good about myself and I am not afraid to enter the working world because of all my experiences in Girl Scouting."

Kelly Frazzini, 13
Lake to River Girl Scout Council
(Ohio)

"... as a Girl Scout, you become aware of the ... outdoor world. The beauty of nature and its splendor not only catches your eye, but captures your heart."

Paula Coleman, 18
Midland Empire Girl Scout Council
(Missouri)

"One gets the feeling that a seeking is going on — girls are seeking for themselves within themselves."

Vicky Trimmer, 17
Hemlock Girl Scout Council, Inc.
(Pennsylvania)

"To me, life is a challenge, and Girl Scouting is my biggest step on the way to meet that challenge."

Vicki Pettit, 15
Great Plains Girl Scout Council, Inc.
(Nebraska)

"Most of all, Girl Scouting lets each girl develop individually. The talents, interests, and even the challenges are different for every girl. All of these help develop the girl as a person by building her personality and character. That is what is most important. The women of today can be themselves, be successful, and love every minute of it."

Brigita Bilsens, 16
Arizona Cactus-Pine Girl Scout Council
(Arizona)

"Girl Scouting gives young girls of today ... a chance to uncover any hidden talents, and a chance to use those talents to their fullest."

Karen Shortt, 16
Dutchess County Girl Scout Council, Inc.
(New York)

"The older you get, the more fun Girl Scouting is."

Linda Carrubba, 15
Nassau Council of Girl Scouts, Inc.
(New York)

"I enjoy the arts because they give me a chance to express myself in a whole new way. ... You don't have to be an expert and, being in Girl Scouts, no one will make fun of you."

Linda Perry, 14
Singing Sands Girl Scout Council, Inc.
(Michigan)

"I still remember earning the ... award; it was the proudest moment of my life and also of my parents'."

Kimberlee Ann Rose, 17
Four Winds Girl Scout Council, Inc.
(Kansas)

Girl Scouting and Group Management Contents

The Girl Scout Promise

On my honor, I will try:
To serve God,
My country and mankind,
And to live by the Girl Scout Law.

The Girl Scout Law

I will do my best:
to be honest
to be fair
to help where I am needed
to be cheerful
to be friendly and considerate
to be a sister to every Girl Scout
to respect authority
to use resources wisely
to protect and improve the world around me
to show respect for myself and others through my words and actions.

Mixed Media, Mik Young Oh, age 15, Mesa, Ariz.

Girl
Scout
Program

Designed for You and by You

You're ready for fun, adventure, and opportunity, for new achievements and relationships with others. You're reaching out for greater competence and independence. You're ready for the best the teen years offer. You're ready for Girl Scouting.

As a Cadette or Senior Girl Scout, you can:

discover more about yourself — your interests, values, and goals;

explore, choose, and build skills for independent living;

go to interesting places and meet people;

express and act upon your cares and hopes for the world;

be recognized for your accomplishments;

share in a worldwide experience.

Cadette or Senior Girl Scouting is for young women, 12 through 17 years of age, of all races, creeds, and ethnic heritages. It is for every teen who seeks new friendships, experiences, and a fulfilling future.

Girl Scouting offers, not a blueprint, but a process that keeps the focus on you. The center of Girl Scouting is the unique you, with talents and potentials different from everyone else, and the you who can share with others.

The journey you map out is your own. Supported by caring adults, you will participate in creating the goals and plans that will guide your activities. You and your leader set the pattern of meetings and build a program that fits your needs.

Within your group, you may choose an independent course of action or one based on working with the group. Whether your direction is individual or group-oriented, you will enjoy the support of belonging. Every Girl Scout offers her special combination of needs, hopes, and experiences. She contributes to the whole of Girl Scouting.

Girl Scouting is flexible within a framework. The amount of time and effort you give to various projects and activities is up to you. This is a judgment you make based on your time, energy, and commitment. As your priorities and interests change, your program changes with you. Because membership offers such a wide variety of things to do, you can create a program that will suit your interests and imagination for years to come.

As a member of Girl Scouts of the United States of America, you are part of a great American family and of an ever-growing international movement that is important in the lives of girls and women all around the world. Today, almost one hundred countries share in Girl Scouting.

From 1912, when Girl Scouting started in the United States, teens like you have reached and grown through Girl Scout activities. While Girl Scout program has expanded to meet the changing needs of time, the basics of its appeal and strength remain the same:

a program that recognizes the importance and worth of each individual member,

member participation in a wide range of activities,

a worldwide scope that recognizes an international sisterhood of girls and women,

the Girl Scout Promise and Law to serve as a guide for personal behavior.

As a member of this national and international community, you have access to ideas and information about activities and events across the country and around the globe. And as a Cadette or Senior Girl Scout you have a chance to attend such events to meet your sister members from around the world.

You have a share in all that Girl Scouting was, is, and can be. You are a part of something designed for you — to involve you now and to help you fashion your future.

The Basics

All the things you do in Girl Scouting, all the things that make up Girl Scout program, have certain common characteristics:

They make the Promise and Law come alive as a guide to action.

They help you grow in the program emphases: deepening your self-awareness, developing skills in relating to others, developing values, and contributing to society.

They increase your knowledge and skills in one or more of the five worlds of interest: the World of Well-Being, the World of People, the World of Today and Tomorrow, the World of the Arts, the World of the Out-of-Doors.

The design on the following page shows the way these key aspects of Girl Scouting fit together.

Girl Scout Program: An Overview

Key Aspects of Girl Scouting Fit Together to Form the Design for Girl Scout Program

The Girl Scout Promise and Law:
The Foundation of Girl Scouting

The Four Program Emphases:
Our Goals for Girls

Five Worlds of Interest:
Activity Areas

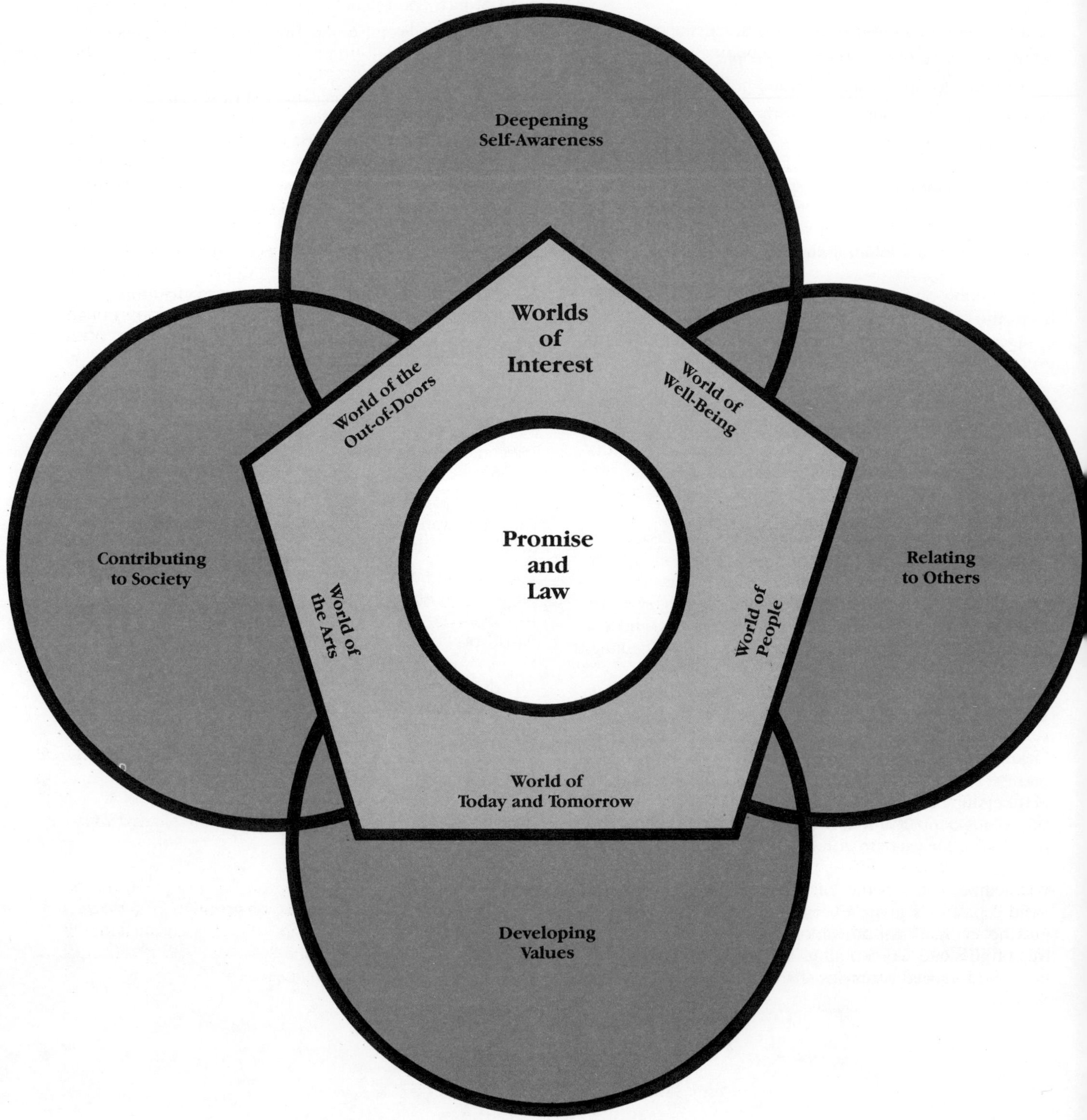

Deepening
Self-Awareness

Worlds
of
Interest

World of the
Out-of-Doors

World of
Well-Being

Contributing
to Society

World of
the Arts

Promise
and
Law

World of
People

Relating
to Others

World of
Today and Tomorrow

Developing
Values

The Possibilities

The basics of program — the Promise and Law, the program emphases, and the worlds of interest — can be combined in many ways. It is as though you are looking at a landscape from different angles. The landscape may stay the same, but the way you see it, the meaning it has for you, changes.

Look at the many ways you can experience the basics of Girl Scouting:

If you want to increase your self-awareness and develop your skills in relating to others and putting your values to work, the Challenge of Being a Girl Scout and the Challenge of Living the Promise and Law are for you. You will find them in the "Challenges: An Invitation to Action" chapter of this book.

Suppose you like to focus on trying things you have never done before, stretching yourself, doing things you like to do, all within a framework of fun? Then, interest projects are for you. You will find them in the "Explore the Worlds of Interest" chapter of this book and in a companion Girl Scout book, *Let's Make It Happen!* (GSUSA, Cat. No. 20–815, 1979).

Are you ready to make the world a better place? to put your ideals into action? Through community and volunteer service, you will discover how and uncover the rewards this brings to others and to yourself. Find out all about opportunities for service in the "Community Service," "Volunteer Service," and "Service in Girl Scouting" chapters of this book.

Maybe you are wondering about your future. Instead of wondering, why not plan? From Dreams to Reality, a career exploration program, which includes an activity book and career cards, will be just the thing to help you on your way to an exciting future. *Let's Make It Happen!* has an interest project in career exploration, too.

If you are ready to take on responsibility and find opportunities to direct and support the efforts of others, you are ready for leadership. Discover ways to take the lead in the "Taking on Leadership" chapter of this book.

Maybe you're saying, "Yes, that's for me," to more than one program possibility. You want to look at program from more than one vantage point. If so, you are ready to combine program possibilities. You may be ready to commit yourself to work on the Girl Scout Silver or Girl Scout Gold Awards — the highest awards in Girl Scouting. The Girl Scout Silver Award symbolizes the highest achievement in Cadette Girl Scouting. The Girl Scout Gold Award is for Seniors and symbolizes the highest award in all Girl Scouting.

The Resources

Program ideas for Cadette and Senior Girl Scouts are contained in more than one publication. To explore all the opportunities available to you and to earn the Girl Scout Silver and Girl Scout Gold Awards, you will want to have access to these companion pieces. Copies may be available from your council's library, or they may be purchased from the Girl Scout department in your local retail store or by mail from the National Equipment Service.

Let's Make It Happen! (GSUSA, Cat. No. 20–815, 1979) is a book with 22 interest projects you can do in a group or individually. You will find fashion, photography, camping, travel, sports, auto maintenance, and more. Guidelines to write projects of your own are also included.

The From Dreams to Reality program includes an activity book, *Adventures in Careers* (GSUSA, Cat. No. 20–810, 1978), and a set of *Career Cards* (GSUSA, Cat. No. 20–811, 1978) designed to help you explore your interests and to relate what you like to do to exciting career choices. Through the 80 women featured on the cards, you will meet and learn how women make plans and decisions related to career and family. Then you will have opportunities to try out your career interests firsthand through internships, trips, paid work, and starting your own business.

Now that you know about the elements of program and the recognitions you can earn, it is time to plan exactly what you want to do. In order to do this, you need to feel comfortable using this book.

You Make the Difference is the key to the opportunities offered to Cadette and Senior Girl Scouts through Girl Scouting. Leaf through this book, referring back to the Contents and to the following chapter as you go along. Begin to get a feeling for the program through the activities you read about. Use it as you would a tour guide — look before you set out on a trip.

You will discover marginal rules to help you find program recommended for your membership level.

A silver rule tells you that the material is especially appropriate for Cadette Girl Scouts.

A blue rule is a sign that the material was designed with a Senior Girl Scout in mind.

In the center of the book you will find a section on the background of Girl Scouting and on group management. It tells you of the proud traditions of Girl Scouting and will help you enhance your chances for fun and good times through successful group management.

Working in groups — especially Girl Scout groups — may be new to you. Or, you may be ready to try activities in leadership development or to earn a volunteer service bar by working with a Girl Scout Group. If so, all of a sudden, group management will be very important. The section called "Girl Scouting and Group Management" will help you over the tough spots and give you ideas to meet the situations you will face. To discover whether your knowledge of Girl Scouting or group management needs a boost, you might try these quizzes. Specific references are on page 70.

Girl Scout Quiz

Are you a whiz at Girl Scout facts and figures? Try your skill at these five teasers. If you get four or more correct, you're doing great. If not, search out answers on pages A-2 through A-18.

1. J.G.L. are the initials of _____, who was the _____.

2. True or false? There are over 300 Girl Scout councils in the United States today.

3. If I wanted to go primitive camping at a Girl Scout national center I could go to _____.

4. WAGGGS stands for _____.

5. Which of these careers cannot be found in Girl Scouting? Accountant, Sales Manager, Writer, Typist, Camp Director.

Group Quiz

Are you great in a group? or are you hesitant? To discover your group "I.Q." try these questions. If you come up blank, look for clues on pages A-19 through A-32.

1. In a girl/adult partnership, the balance of responsibility is determined by _____.

2. The group representative system is like the _____ system in Girl Scouting.

3. When you _____, you are in a helping role and when you _____, you are in a hindering role.

4. When is a questionnaire useful? _____

5. When would you use the group process? _____, _____, _____ .

Putting It All Together

Print, Evelyn Cohen, age 14, Potomac, Md.

The following chapters tell about new program elements that you can put together to suit your particular interests. To help you find your way, here are some possible interest areas with answers about what each one can offer.

Career Exploration

Where are the information and requirements?
Information about career exploration can be found in *From Dreams to Reality: Adventures in Careers; From Dreams to Reality: Career Cards;* and in *Let's Make It Happen!* on page 15, the Career Exploration interest project.

Whom is it designed for?
In *From Dreams to Reality: Adventures in Careers,* the activities marked with one circle are designed for Cadette Girl Scouts, the activities marked with two circles are designed for Senior Girl Scouts. In *Let's Make It Happen!,* the career exploration project is suitable for both levels of Girl Scouting.

What is the earned recognition?
The program outlined in *From Dreams to Reality: Adventures in Careers* can lead to an activity certificate, a pilots certificate, an award letter, and a From Dreams to Reality Pilots pin. A From Dreams to Reality patch is also available. The project in *Let's Make It Happen!* leads to an interest project certificate and patch.

Challenges

Where are the information and requirements?
Information about Challenges can be found in the "Challenges: An Invitation to Action" chapter of this book.

Whom are they designed for?
There are two Challenges: the Challenge of Being a Girl Scout is recommended for Cadette Girl Scouts; the Challenge of Living the Promise and Law is recommended for Senior Girl Scouts.

What is the earned recognition?
Each Challenge has its own pin.

The Girl Scout Silver Award and the Girl Scout Gold Award

Where are the information and requirements?
Information about these awards can be found in the "The Highest Awards in Girl Scouting" chapter of this book.

Whom are they designed for?
The Girl Scout Silver Award is designed for Cadette Girl Scouts. The Girl Scout Gold Award is the highest achievement in Girl Scouting. You must be at least 14 years old or a Senior Girl Scout to begin to work toward it.

What is the earned recognition?
Each award has its own pin.

Interest Projects

Where are the information and requirements?
Information about interest projects can be found in *Let's Make It Happen!* and in the "Explore the Worlds of Interest" chapter of this book.

Whom are they designed for?
All the interest projects are suitable for both Girl Scout levels. If you have a special interest, not covered by a project, see *Let's Make It Happen!*, page 69. Younger Cadettes may also earn the 32 tan badges in *Girl Scout Badges and Signs* (GSUSA, Cat. No. 20–711, 1980).

What is the earned recognition?
Each project has its own certificate and patch.

Leadership

Where are the information and requirements?
Information about leadership can be found in the "Taking on Leadership" chapter of this book.

Whom is it designed for?
The Silver Leadership Award is designed for Cadette Girl Scouts; the Gold Leadership Award is designed for Senior Girl Scouts.

What is the earned recognition?
Each award has its own pin.

Service

Where are the information and requirements?
Information about service can be found in the "Community Service," "Volunteer Service," and "Service in Girl Scouting" chapters of this book.

Whom is it designed for?
The community service project is designed for Cadette Girl Scouts. The volunteer service projects are recommended for Senior Girl Scouts.

What is the earned recognition?
The community service project has no separate insignia. The volunteer service projects can lead to a volunteer service bar (one for each of the five worlds and one for Girl Scouting), a certificate, and a letter.

The Ten-Year Award

This award recognizes the dedication and commitment of the individual girl who completes ten years of Girl Scouting. The years need not be consecutive. The award is available only to girls.

On Your Own

To get started, make a list of the things that appeal to you as you look over all the program materials. Your list might look like this:

Program Element	Activity	Page Number	Want to Earn Recognition
Challenge of Being a Girl Scout	All sections	33	Yes
World of Today and Tomorrow Interest Project	Spread the Word, Nightwatch	52	Undecided — need 8 or more activities.
World of the Out-of-Doors Interest Project	Take Care!	58	Yes — will find other activities to do. Talk to group members.
From Dreams to Reality: Adventures in Careers	It's Up to You, Blankety Blank	25 49	Undecided

Next, spend some time discovering how the activities you chose match the requirements of the Silver Award or the Gold Award (depending on your Girl Scout level). If you have a variety of program elements, you may discover that completing these choices will put you part of the way toward earning one of these awards. A highest recognition may be closer than you think.

Get Your Group Together

Before your plan is set, check with your group members to discover who has similar interests. Maybe others have chosen something that will appeal to you too, once you have discussed it with them. Can you form a group to carry out activities? Often that's the most fun. You might make a list of where your choices match:

Program Element	Group Members Involved	Working Toward Recognition
The Challenge of Being a Girl Scout	Judy, Sharon, Carmen, Joan	Yes — All
World of the Arts Interest Project	Cecilia, Joan, Michelle	Yes — All
World of the Out-of-Doors Interest Project	Carmen, Patricia Kathy, Velma, Anne-Marie	Yes No

Once you know where your interests coincide, you can plan what to do together. Try to coordinate your activities to get the right balance and number of activities going at any one time. You will need to weigh the urge everyone has to do her choice first, against the need to pick a manageable number of activities that won't overtax the group's members, or the adults who share the action.

A good way to tell if you have planned realistically is to try out your program scheme for a short period of time. Then decide if the plan is worth the energy it takes, compared to the satisfaction it brings.

If the members of your group all plan to do several elements of program, such as Challenges and interest projects, you might assign small teams to study each option thoroughly and recommend a way of carrying out activities to the larger group. On the other hand, you might find that some members of your group want to combine parts of program, while others want to focus on one part, such as career exploration or service. That's fine as long as each person works in a team, when appropriate, and has a clear grasp of what she is doing.

A very important element to the success of any group where different things are happening at once is to keep everyone informed. This can be done verbally, on a regular basis, at the beginning of each group meeting. But, as a reminder, it's good to have things in writing, too. One way to assure that everyone knows the group's plans is to write your proposed activities on a calendar. The Long-Run Calendar in the "Forming a Group" section will show you how to do this.

A second element in effective communication calls for individual record-keeping. Use the following Program Planning Agreement to specify what you plan to do and how you plan to do it. You can use this to record your plan for doing activities within a program element, or for earning a recognition or a highest award. Be as specific in the agreement as you can, remembering that you can change it as you go along to fit new conditions or to get over a trouble spot.

Program Planning Agreement

Name(s):_____

Program Element:_____

Time Frame: _____ hrs.   FROM_____TO_____

Description or Activity	What I (We) Will Do	Resources/ Consultants Needed	Projected Completion Date	Projected Time	Actual Time

Times to talk over plans/progress: _____ with _____

_____ with _____   _____ with _____

Agreement made

Signed:_____and_____and_____
                                    leader   if any
                                                                        consultant(s)

_____

_____

_____

_____
girl participant(s)

_____completed on_____
Program element   date

Signed:_____and_____and_____
                                    leader   if any
                                                                        consultant(s)

_____

_____

_____

_____
girl participant(s)

_____date_____
Note changes of plans here

_____date_____
Note changes of plans here

In addition to writing down each part of program that you do, keep a record of your overall accomplishments using the Program Progress Chart, which follows. This will give a total picture of where you have been, where you are now, and where you are going. It is particularly important if you change groups, move in and out of special interest groups, work on recognitions in council events or camp program, or experience a change in adult leadership of your group. Should you decide to work toward the Girl Scout Silver Award and/or the Girl Scout Gold Award, it is necessary to show your progress and to record how you met each of the requirements.

There are several different ways that you can be a member and participate in Girl Scouting, so you needn't wonder about being in an area where there are few girls your age or few who share your interests.

Forming an interest group is a way of organizing a number of girls, who, along with you, may share similar goals or abilities. These groups may be formed separately from your regular troop. Interest groups can consist of individuals, girls from within a troop, and/or members of several troops.

Events, workshops, trips, and various opportunities offered by Girl Scouts throughout the year make it possible for you to pursue your individual interests, yet keep your lines of communication open with other Girl Scouts. This way you can gain from program opportunities, even if you are not a member of a troop or interest group.

Even within the traditional troop structure, you can find variations. For example, in communities where there are few girls, the troop may include more than one age level.

Whatever way you join in the many activities and experiences of Girl Scouting, you will have the support of other Girl Scouts.

Program Progress Chart

_____

Name _____

Council _____

Record from _____ to _____

Troop(s)   Leader(s)

_____

_____

	Date Begun	Description of Activities	Completed
The Challenge of Being a Girl Scout			
The Challenge of Living the Promise and Law			
Religious Recognition			
(specify)			
American Indian Tradition Award			
Girl Scout tan badges			
(specify)			
Interest Projects			
(specify)			

	Date Begun	Description of Activities	Completed

Community Service Projects

(specify)

Volunteer Service

(specify)

LIT Training

CIT Training

***From Dreams to Reality: Adventures in Careers* Activities**

(specify)

Pilots Activities

(specify)

Silver Leadership Award

(specify)

Gold Leadership Award

(specify)

Girl Scout Silver Award

Girl Scout Gold Award

Other

Drawing, Brenda Robinson, age 16, Altamonte Springs, Fla.

Community Service

You look all around you and you see things that need doing: in your neighborhood, in your school, in your country, for people. You don't want things just to happen to you. You want to make things happen, things that count. You want to do something!

So what can you do about it?

You can give up and hope someone else will solve the problems. You can say, "I don't care." Or, you can *Do something.* But what? how? where do you start?

Look around you and see where you can make a difference using your special skills and your commitment.

If you want to start something new in your school, town, or neighborhood, or perhaps stop something, how will you go about letting people know about your idea? Who will help you get action started? What are some of the problems you might face?

This list may give you some idea of project areas:
adults
animals
buildings
children
drugs
the elderly
employment
hunger
loneliness
parks
people with disabilities
personal dignity
physical fitness
playgrounds
pollution
privacy
recreation
sick people
streets
urban blight
violence

Focus your ideas: What do you want to be different than it is now — because of you and others?

Pick out some one thing you'd like to do. If your ideas change along the way, that's all right. You have to start somewhere. Everybody does.

Begin your planning by answering the following:

One thing that really needs doing that I (we) can do is:

_____

_____

Things are this way now: _____

_____

Things could be like this: _____

_____

Some ways I (we) could make this happen are: _____

_____

_____

To make my idea work, I need to: plan my strategy before I plunge in, and have my action ideas, something I really want to do.

To do what you want to do, to get things moving, you may have to overcome many obstacles, change direction, try new approaches.

Consider how you might handle situations when someone says:
"Your ideas won't work."
"I'm too busy to see you now!"
"There is a law against it."
"We don't want your help."

Chances are you'll need some help. Get the best help and advice you can. List people who can help you — people who can open doors for you to sell your idea, recruit other people to help, and clear red tape. Include their names, addresses, and telephone numbers.

Now you are ready to go ahead, to do something. Spell out your plan so everyone knows who does what and when. Then do it! the best way you know how.

And don't forget, let others know what you are doing. Who needs to know?

Write letters to your local newspaper, or print a newspaper or newssheet of your own to tell the world what you are doing and why.

Talk to people. Explain your ideas, what you are trying to do. Ask for their help.

The rest is up to you. Don't just stand there. *Do* something!

22

Financing Your Plans

Generally, a community service project can be carried out within the troop's budget. But what about those beautiful, far-out ideas you have? those tremendous plans for ways to make your community a safer, healthier, happier, and more beautiful place? What will happen to those ideas if your troop budget is down to zero?

If your project calls for financial resources that you don't have, you might want to plan a money-earning project. In some cases you may want to seek co-sponsors of your project among other groups in the community. Your first step is to contact your council through your leader to get approval of your plans.

Help may be as close as your troop sponsor. Many businesses and service groups would be more than willing to join you — if they knew about your project. Make an appointment to visit their meeting to tell them about your plans, what you would like to do, and how you want to go about it. Ask for their suggestions, as well as their help. Who knows what the outcome might be? One Senior Girl Scout troop approached its sponsor with plans to create a nursery and playroom at the new women's center. The Senior Girl Scouts not only got the help they needed, but the sponsor took on equipping a kitchen for the center as well.

Be original in your approach! A council planning board suggested creating a physical fitness trail in a city park. The council got help from the early morning joggers who stopped to read the eye-catching posters along their way.

Your Girl Scout council office, your library, or your local chamber of commerce can also provide information about community groups whose interests and concerns are similar to yours. "We never knew about this service club before," wrote one Cadette Girl Scout, "until the librarian heard about our plans. With her suggestion, our council went to work. Guess what? Our plans matched the club's concerns so we joined forces in a project, instead of operating a similar effort a few blocks down the street."

Reader's Digest Foundation Grants

A very special fund available only to Cadette and Senior Girl Scouts is the Reader's Digest Foundation Grants to Girl Scouts for Community Service.

Storefront tutoring centers, drug education efforts, swimming classes for people with disabilities, senior citizen centers, and job placement bureaus are only a few of the kinds of projects funded with this grant.

Often, a Reader's Digest Foundation Grant to Girl Scouts has been "seed money" unlocking community funds not available before. Sometimes the funding makes it possible for girls to launch a project "everyone said was impossible," or to "show what Girl Scouts are capable of doing, if given the chance."

To apply for a grant, you fill out the application that is included each year in the annual GSUSA publication, *Runways,* telling why there is a need for this project at this time and just how your plans will meet that need. In the application, you describe in your own words the people, skills, time, and money the project will require. You set the date for beginning the project and promise to submit a complete report of the activity and a financial report at the end of the grant period, if you are funded. Ask someone in your Girl Scout council office for more information on how and when to apply.

Pencil Drawing, Joseph Dimattia, age 17, Wichita, Kans

Volunteer Service

What would happen if there were no volunteers to offer their services in the U.S.A. and around the world? For one thing, there would be no Girl Scout troops. Volunteers work in many organizations and capacities. They staff youth organizations, help in hospitals, raise funds for musical organizations, work with juvenile offenders, beautify parks, and fill many other needs.

Teenagers, too, can serve as volunteers.

Girl Scout Volunteer Service is an apprenticeship program where girls learn how to carry out this important community responsibility.

Each girl in a volunteer service project has the opportunity to utilize or to be trained in specific skills and then to demonstrate her own potential. As a Girl Scout service volunteer, you become a resource for your community and an agent for positive change.

The volunteer service project is set up in conjunction with your council, or another agency or organization, or other community resources in your area. To find out what volunteer service projects are available at the present time, check your Girl Scout council. Once you have discussed and chosen a project with your leader and council, the necessary arrangements with the cooperating agency or organization will be made.

A volunteer service project is something that you take part in as an individual. You may be working on your project alone, or with other people, but the decision to participate is made by each individual. It gives you a chance to explore a field that interests you. You receive training, either before you start or on the job. Doing a volunteer service project means that you want to volunteer your services, not be paid for them.

Volunteer service projects can be another means of exploring certain careers. They are skill-building projects where you gain much valuable knowledge. But they also give something invaluable to others, something that they wouldn't have if there weren't volunteers like you.

In choosing a volunteer service project, you must consider the resources available to you through your council and through your community. You and the group you are helping need to work out the specific details of your project: a beginning date, a training program, the materials needed, transportation arrangements, dress codes (where applicable), working papers, hours, and the agreed-upon length of service. You may want your leader's advice, too.

As a service volunteer, you are required to:

be a registered Girl Scout,

meet the age and/or grade requirements established by the training and/or service organization,

take special orientation or training for the service,

make a commitment to give a minimum of 25 hours of service following training.

When you complete your service training, you will be eligible for a service bar, which may be worn when you are giving service and may be worn on your Girl Scout uniform. (See "Cadette and Senior Girl Scout Recognitions" for correct placement of this insignia.) One or more volunteer service bars can be earned in Girl Scouting and in each of the five worlds of interest.

When you complete 25 hours of service, you will receive a volunteer service certificate and a letter written by your council, leader, or a person from the group where you volunteered service. This letter and certificate can be used as a reference when you apply for a job and when you apply for further education.

You can help a great deal by volunteering 25 hours of service, but it is hoped you won't stop there. There is never an upper limit to the amount of service you can give. Who knows? This volunteer opportunity may lead to a long-term commitment as a volunteer or to a paid job and an exciting career.

If you want to continue your volunteer service, consider using the opportunity to widen your experience and to grow on the job. Talk to the supervisor of your volunteer service project or to your leader. To earn a second volunteer service bar for the same service project, you must take additional training and work an additional 25 hours.

Service in Girl Scouting

Textile Design, Eva Detsis, age 18, St. Petersburg, Fla.

Do you enjoy being a Girl Scout? Do you want to share the skills you have learned in troop and camp with younger Girl Scouts? Do you want to help tell the Girl Scout story so others will listen, join, or help? If so, you have still more volunteer service possibilities.

Volunteer your services to your own Girl Scout council as a Girl Scout program volunteer (sometimes called a program aide) in a troop or camp unit, as a Leader-in-Training (LIT), or a Counselor-in-Training (CIT). Assist with the maintenance of council facilities or equipment; be trained for a speakers' bureau; or help develop visual aids, program, and training tools; or assist in the writing and layout of the council bulletin and annual report.

Your Girl Scout volunteer service will be developed by your own council or, in some instances, with another council or Girl Scout group.

Leader-in-Training

Leader-in-Training is a challenging opportunity to share the skills you learn and the fun you have as a Girl Scout.

The qualifications to be a Leader-in-Training are:

be an active registered Girl Scout of your troop,

be 16 or 17 years of age, or have completed your sophomore year in high school,

be in good health,

have experience working with children,

have a real interest in the progress and welfare of younger Girl Scouts.

A Leader-in-Training completes a group leadership course while apprenticing as a leader in a Brownie, Junior, or Cadette troop. An LIT project extends over a five- to eight-month period, with the time divided between course sessions and actual work with a troop.

Talk over your qualifications with your leader and, if you both agree you could qualify, file an application with your council office according to your council's procedures.

Counselor-in-Training

A Counselor-in-Training project gives you the opportunity to work with children in the out-of-doors and to acquire valuable on-the-job experience. Training for counselor work is given in Girl Scout camps.

The qualifications to be a Counselor-in-Training are:

meet all the qualifications required, or have completed a Leader-in-Training project;

be advanced enough in camping skills to be able to teach them to others;

have at least eight weeks of resident, troop, or day camping, or four weeks, plus other comparable experience, acceptable to your council;

have serious intentions of becoming a camp counselor or camp specialist.

A Counselor-in-Training completes an outdoor group leadership course while apprenticing as a counselor in a Girl Scout camp. The training includes regular hours devoted to classes, plus apprenticeship in camp units working directly with the children. The cost for this training will vary with councils, but you should expect to pay regular camper fees during your stay in camp.

Some councils make it possible for Senior Girl Scouts to accomplish Leader-in-Training and Counselor-in-Training within a year. The plan generally includes five to eight months as a Leader-in-Training during the fall, winter, or spring, to be followed in the summer with a four-week Counselor-in-Training course.

Watercolor, Karen Marselle, age 14, Hoffman Estates, Ill.

TAKING ON LEADERSHIP

Leadership is the spark that can ignite action, release each person's unique creative potential, and keep a group moving toward its goals. Leadership isn't confined to just those people who have been elected to office or appointed to a title. Leadership is a way of thinking and acting that anyone can try. That leadership spark can come from you.

Make leadership work for your group. First, agree that you won't keep leadership concentrated in one or a few individuals whom you depend on all the time. Instead, decide to share responsibilities and help leadership skills grow among all members of your group. This sharing of leadership roles can give you a greater feeling of accomplishment from belonging to a group and give you greater freedom to concentrate on doing the things you want to do, confident in the expectation that everyone is pitching in to move things ahead.

Good leadership takes skills that are admired and needed in the world today. There is no better place to learn and sharpen those skills than in your Girl Scout group, where people will try to be understanding and sympathetic to your efforts. You can watch what other leaders do, both your friends and the adults involved in your group. And you can learn by doing, benefiting from your successes and your mistakes. Now is the time for you to discover your own ideas about leadership, as you develop your leadership qualities and practice leadership skills.

All groups have leaders for different things at many different times. There are many ways to determine leaders and each way can fit a particular situation. Try different ways each time you need someone to take the lead. Here are some suggestions and, as you get going, you'll be able to add your own:

appoint a committee

call for volunteers

count off by number

elect by vote

keep a "Kaper Chart"

pick by chance

share by pairs

take turns by alphabet

Who are the leaders? What a "real" leader is seems to depend a lot on what people expect a leader to be, or on what they are looking for at any given time. That's one reason so many different people can be leaders at so many different times.

What kinds of qualities do you look for in a leader? Think of four people you know (or know about) whom you would describe as good leaders. For each of these, identify some of the personal qualities or characteristics that this person has and that you admire. Write ten words that describe each of these four people.

Now look at the total picture. What are the similar qualities that you admire about all four leaders? Do you know any people who have some of these characteristics but are not good leaders? Why is this so? Which of these qualities do you have or want? What about other people in your group?

Develop a picture of your ideal leader. Individually, or as a small or total group, sort out the necessary ingredients for being a good leader. Decide whether you or members of your group fit this outline and how you can grow to fulfill such a role.

What do leaders do? Leaders take care of things that need doing so the group can act and keep going. They get other members of the group involved and they get things done.

Take the leadership inventory from the "Calculate Your Skills" activity, found in *Let's Make It Happen!* (pages 42–43). This inventory lists some of the things leaders do. Rarely does one person do all these things in a group. Each person has different skills and experiences and, if only one or two persons carry out all these functions, there is a risk other members will lose interest or their sense of belonging to the group. When leadership shifts back and forth among group members, you can meet many different needs. Use the inventory to discover your leadership needs and potentials. You can use all your group's activities and experiences to date, or a specific group project, as your basis for the inventory.

Check the inventory points now, or over a period of time, to see which leadership functions are being carried out, which need strengthening, and who your leaders are.

Ask certain people to be observers of a particular activity. Have them fill in the inventory and share their findings with the group.

Use the inventory as a personal checklist. Have each person check her own copy whenever she sees herself functioning as a leader in any of the ways listed.

You and Your Group's Adult Leader

You and your adult leader work together in a partnership aimed at making the most of all your experiences. She/he has volunteered to help you and your group achieve your goals and to find satisfaction in your efforts and accomplishments. She/he is there to listen, support, suggest, guide, and act as a resource for you as you create the kind of programs that best fit your needs and interests.

Your adult leader is your resource in the leadership and management of your group. The leadership roles adults carry can differ from group to group and can change within the group itself according to the wishes, needs, and experiences of the members. How much direct leadership she/he takes, for example, will depend a lot on how much leadership the other group members are willing and able to carry.

How many of the things that your leader does are you ready to do? To find out, individually or with your group, identify and inventory what she/he does as a leader. Use this leadership inventory every few months to discover how your adult leader's activities change, depending on what program you are doing, and how your readiness to take on adult leadership responsibilities changes over time. After each task your leader does, decide where you would stand handling the same responsibility: Have you already done it? are you ready to do it now? could you do it with some training? or, is it something you're not ready for yet?

Once you have completed this inventory, decide with your leader how you could take over or join her/him in carrying out leadership responsibilities. Arrange to get the training necessary to do your leadership job effectively.

To develop your leadership skills in depth, consider earning the Silver or Gold Leadership Award. The Silver Award is designed especially for Cadette Girl Scouts. The Gold Award is designed particularly with Senior Girl Scouts in mind.

Silver Leadership Award

The Silver Leadership Award calls for you to develop and evaluate your skills as a leader. You must spend at least 25 hours on one of the following activities, **or** on a combination of the activities, to earn this recognition.

Earn a certificate for one or more of the following interest projects in *Let's Make It Happen!*: Leadership (pages 42–45), Emergency Preparedness (pages 27–29), or Outdoor Survival (pages 50–52). Document and evaluate your experiences.

(**Note:** If you complete one or more of these interest projects to earn the Silver Leadership Award, it (they) may not count as part of the interest projects you do to earn the Girl Scout Silver Award and/or the Girl Scout Gold Award.)

Serve a term as an officer in your group. Document and evaluate your experiences.

Earn a Girl Scout volunteer service bar by working as a program volunteer in a troop of younger girls (for a period of at least three months) or at a resident or day camp (for a two-week period). Document and evaluate your experiences.

(**Note:** If you earn a Girl Scout volunteer service bar for this award, it may not count for the Challenge of Living the Promise and Law as well. If you have earned two volunteer service bars for the same service project, the second bar could count toward this award. See page 25 for details.)

Plan and carry out the bridging activities for a Junior Girl Scout troop. Document and evaluate your experiences.

Take charge of planning a major trip or special event for your group. Evaluate your experiences afterward.

Gold Leadership Award

You are in the spotlight now, on your way to becoming a model of the effective group leader. To earn the Gold Leadership Award, the outward symbol of your skills, you must do one or more of the following activities, spending at least 25 hours on one or a combination of them within a four-month period. Document your experiences and your discoveries about leadership with your group and with your group leader.

Serve as an officer of your Girl Scout group.

Complete LIT or CIT training and assist with a younger group of girls.

After receiving training, use your skills to train leaders of younger girls.

Serve on a Senior Planning Board (or its equivalent in your council, if possible).

Serve in a leadership capacity in your school, community, house of worship, or other community or youth organization.

Serve with adults on a council committee or council board of directors, if your state law permits, or serve as a delegate to the National Council.

Cadette and Senior Girl Scout Recognitions

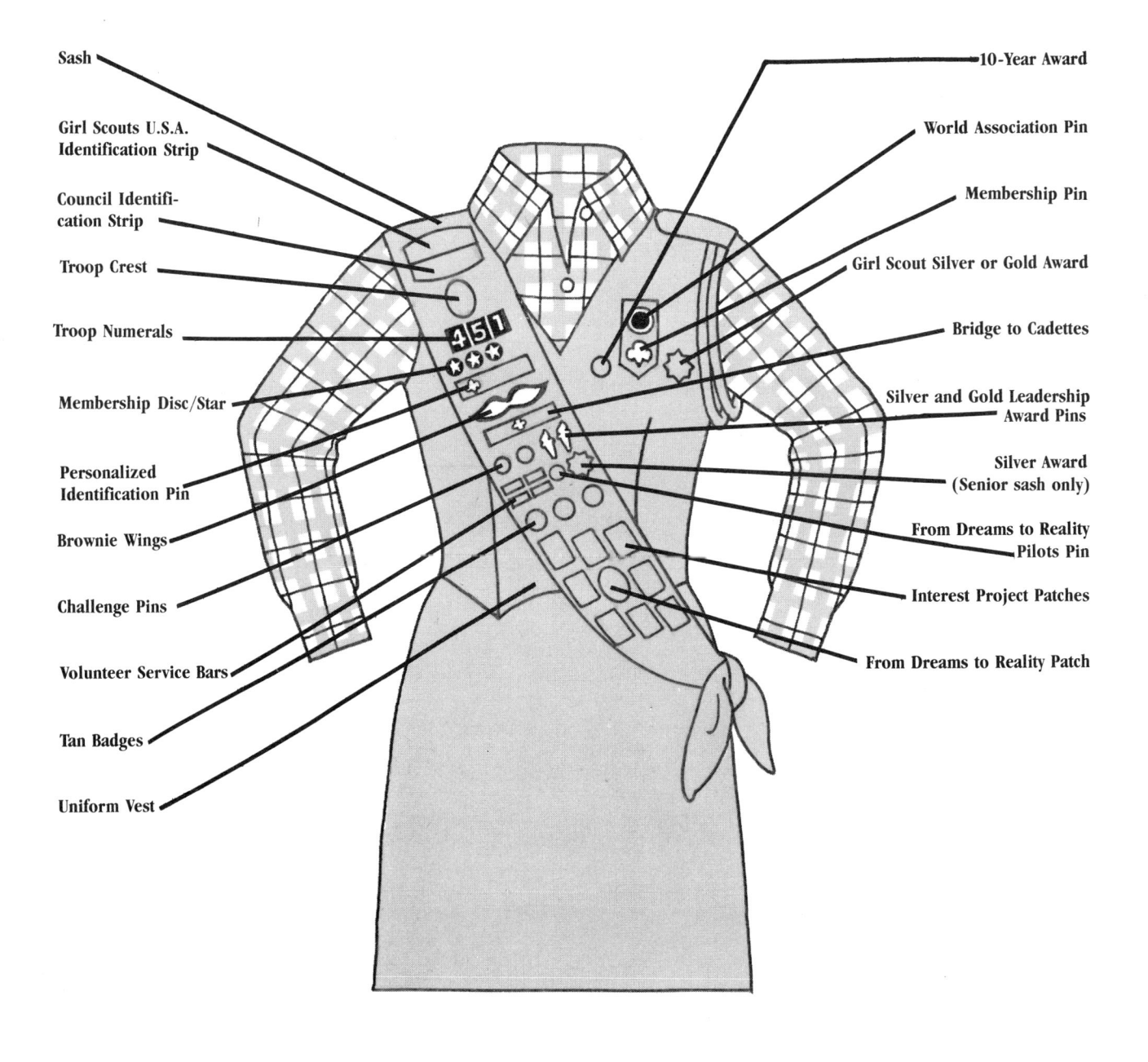

Sash

Girl Scouts U.S.A. Identification Strip

Council Identification Strip

Troop Crest

Troop Numerals

Membership Disc/Star

Personalized Identification Pin

Brownie Wings

Challenge Pins

Volunteer Service Bars

Tan Badges

Uniform Vest

10-Year Award

World Association Pin

Membership Pin

Girl Scout Silver or Gold Award

Bridge to Cadettes

Silver and Gold Leadership Award Pins

Silver Award (Senior sash only)

From Dreams to Reality Pilots Pin

Interest Project Patches

From Dreams to Reality Patch

CHALLENGES: An Invitation to Action

Ink Drawing, Barbara Bennett, age 18, Indianapolis, Ind.

What are Challenges? The dictionary defines a challenge as an invitation to a game or contest. There are two Challenges for Cadette and Senior Girl Scouts. Each is an invitation to you to test your performance in actual projects in your community. Each asks you to deepen your understanding of yourself, of others, and to find the unique ways you can contribute to the well-being of your community. When you decide to work on these recognitions you accept the challenges of putting the ideals of Girl Scouting into action and taking on a commitment, which might last an entire troop year. If you think you are really ready to test yourself, tackle a Challenge:

The Challenge of Being a Girl Scout helps you understand more about yourself and how the ideals of Girl Scouting relate to your everyday life. Most girls will choose to work on this Challenge first.

The Challenge of Living the Promise and Law calls on you to set goals for yourself, to make commitments to yourself and others, to put your values into action, and to take a step into your own future.

When you have completed a Challenge you will receive an insignia to wear on your uniform. It is a symbol of your readiness to take action and of your inner strength.

The Challenge of Being a Girl Scout

Being a Girl Scout, representing and standing up for all that Girl Scouting means, can be quite a challenge and responsibility, but it is worth it. As a Girl Scout, you are challenged to be the best possible person you can be. This involves knowing yourself, relating well to other people, and being responsible for your actions. The Challenge of Being a Girl Scout is a guide to help you as you discover more about yourself — you the person and the Girl Scout.

The Challenge of Being a Girl Scout has five sections: four preps (short for "preparation steps") and a Challenge. Preps are designed to help you prepare to do the Challenge.

To earn this Challenge, complete the questions, activity, and summary for each of the four preps and then the final Challenge. The preps can be done in any order. You may work on several at one time or do each of them separately. They may be done with others in your troop, or you may work on them alone and discuss them with your troop leader or program consultant.

After you have completed the four preps, you are ready to put what you have discovered to work for yourself and others. Now you can meet the challenge of contributing to the well-being of your community in a way that puts your knowledge of the Girl Scout Promise and Law into action. The Challenge takes the form of a community service project, which may be done with others or alone, if you choose.

When you have completed the four preps and the Challenge, you and your leader decide whether you have successfully met the Challenge of Being a Girl Scout using the "You Decide Guide" found on page 38.

Prep 1: Knowing About Girl Scouting

Find the answers to these questions before doing the activities.

What is WAGGGS? Who belongs?

What are the locations of the world centers?

Find out about at least two member countries of the World Association of Girl Guides and Girl Scouts.

What do Girl Guides do for their communities?

Find out about the variety of volunteer and paid positions in your Girl Scout council.

Find out who your council's delegates to the National Council Session are and what they do there.

What are the special aspects of both Cadette and Senior Girl Scouting?

In what ways are your religious beliefs similar to the Girl Scout Promise and Law?

What do you like best about being a Girl Scout?

How did Girl Scouting begin? when and by whom?

What is the Juliette Low World Friendship Fund and what is it used for?

Select one of the following activities or design one of your own that shows you have knowledge of Girl Scouting, its purpose, and history.

Design an activity that will help others know about the Girl Scout organization and WAGGGS. Prepare all the equipment needed, and set up and use the activity with the persons you choose. (Include facts about GSUSA, WAGGGS, national and international centers, history of the Girl Scout organization.)

OR

Using *The Wide World of Girl Guiding and Girl Scouting* (GSUSA, Cat. No. 19–713, 1980) as a model, prepare a booklet or presentation for younger girls on at least two other countries that are members of the World Association. *Trefoil Round the World* (WAGGGS, Cat. No. 23–962, revised 1978) is a handy reference for information. Add material that would tell girls about Girl Scouts/Girl Guides and everyday life in each of the countries.

OR

Write a biography, series of poems or songs, a fictionalized account, a play, or choreograph a dance on important people in the history of the Girl Scout movement.

OR

Follow a council staff member, camp staff person, or volunteer for at least several hours. Assist her as much as possible and learn about her work and Girl Scouting as a profession or avocation.

OR

Do volunteer work at your Girl Scout council office for at least several hours, assisting with the regular work or with a special project.

Here are some things I discovered about Girl Scouting in the United States: _____

_____

_____

_____

_____.

Here are some things I discovered about Girl Guiding: _

_____

_____

_____.

I shared my new knowledge this way(s): _____

_____

_____.

Date:_____

Prep 2: Knowing Myself Better

By yourself, or with others, complete the inventory below by thinking through an answer to the questions or discussing them with others.

What do I like to do best?

What can I do well?

Which of these can I do better than most people?

What would I like to do better?

What do I do poorly?

What new things would I like to try?

What new things have I tried lately?

What would I like to stop doing?

Whom do I admire and why?

How well do I keep physically fit?

Do my eating habits match nutrition standards?

Am I satisfied with my physical dimensions?

What do I feel is important about the way I present myself to others?

What makes me happy, sad, afraid, excited, angry, frustrated, silly?

What makes me feel good about myself?

What way do I feel hurt by others?

What ways do I sometimes hurt others?

What makes me feel the most emotional?

What makes me feel most in control of myself and my actions?

Select one of the following activities or design one of your own that helps you to know yourself better.

Make a list of qualities you value in a friend. Mark those qualities you already possess. Choose one or two qualities you would like to have. Over a three- to four-week period, make every effort to make these qualities your own.

OR

Try something new, a new skill or activity. Find out who could help you in gaining a new skill and seek out their help. Spend at least five hours trying something new to you.

OR

Try two or more activities in the Fashion/Fitness/Makeup Interest Project (see *Let's Make It Happen!*, page 33) to change or improve your overall appearance.

New discoveries about myself: _____

_____

_____

_____

_____

_____

_____.

Something I want to change/try is: _____

_____

_____

_____

_____.

I tried this activity: _____

_____

_____

_____

_____

_____

_____

_____.

Date: _____

Prep 3: Relating to Others Better

Answer these questions on your own or with others.

What ways do I show friendship?

What ways do I express love?

What do I do to make others happy?

In what ways do I use each of these to show what I mean: my voice, my gestures, my posture, my spoken words, my clothing and accessories, my makeup and hairdo, and my care of belongings at home?

What things do I enjoy doing with others? by myself?

What type of encouragement from others helps me feel good about myself?

How do I give encouragement to others?

Whom do I go to if I need someone to listen to me?

Whom do I go to if I need help?

How do I take on leadership in a group?

How do I include others in making decisions?

Do one of the activities below or design your own activity in which skills relating to other people are important.

Plan and carry out an outing or party for family, hospital patients, senior citizens, or a group in your community.

Practice your skills as hostess and cook. Help everyone to feel comfortable and have a grand time.

OR

Plan and carry out a coed event, such as a day of sports or backpacking, a debate, or a party. Include boys on the planning committee.

Practice good listening skills.

Think of "get acquainted" games and activities to involve everyone in the project.

OR

Do one of the following activities from the interest projects in *Let's Make It Happen!*:

"Communicate in Crisis," page 28.

"Getting Over the Hard Spots," page 19.

"Passing Down a Tradition," page 38.

"Reach Out," page 40.

"Traveler's Aid," page 59.

Here are ways I relate well to others: _____

_____

_____

_____

_____

This is how I would like to improve: _____

_____

_____

_____

_____

I did the following activity: _____

_____

_____

_____

_____

Date: _____

Prep 4: Developing Values for Living

Answer these questions on your own or with others.

What is a value?

What do I feel most strongly about?

What values am I now trying to establish for myself?

What values am I not sure about?

What values are hardest for me to live by?

Have I ever consented to do something I really didn't believe in? Did I feel a sense of conflict? How did I resolve this feeling?

How do the points of view, customs, and traditions of my family, ethnic group, racial group, and religious group influence me?

What parts of the Girl Scout Law do I value most?

What parts am I able to act upon regularly?

What parts are most difficult to act upon?

Take an active part in planning and carrying out a Girl Scouts' Own which demonstrates the ways the Girl Scout Promise and Law help you show your feelings about serving God and your country and your pledge to be a good citizen. (See the "Ceremonies: Special to Girl Scouting" section for information about a Girl Scouts' Own.)

I did the following for a Girl Scouts' Own: _____

_____

_____

_____

_____

The part(s) of the Girl Scouts' Own I found most important:

_____

_____

_____

_____

_____

_____

_____

Date: _____

The Challenge

Here is your Challenge. It uses what you have learned in the four prep sections. Your Challenge is to do something for your community in which you give something of yourself and make a significant impact by your efforts to serve others. Look over the "Community Service" chapter for help on deciding what might be done and how to get started. You may choose how you wish to contribute to your community by following these steps to success:

Select a project to become involved in.

Review what you can bring to the project by going over the prep questions in the knowing myself, relating to others, and developing values sections of this Challenge. What are you good at? How do you work best with others? What's most important to you?

Plan every step of your project. (See the "Getting Together" chapter for help in planning.)

Carry out your project.

Evaluate your Challenge project:

> Did you accomplish what you set out to do?
>
> In what way(s) did your Challenge project have an impact on others?
>
> In what way(s) did you give of yourself?
>
> How does what you did relate to the ideals of Girl Scouting?
>
> How would you improve what you did?

Here are some successful project ideas from Girl Scouts all over the country. Try one, or design your own way to meet a need in your community:

In the World of Well-Being, organize a children's sports day, assist at a community New Games festival, or at a Special Olympics (for the disabled).

In the World of People, assist as a literacy volunteer; help with programs for refugee peoples; help spread the word about getting out to vote, immunization, food stamps, etc.

In the World of Today and Tomorrow, serve as an audiovisual assistant in your school, troop, council, house of worship; be a math or science tutor.

In the World of the Arts, teach crafts to children, work on an art project with senior citizens, provide arts activities in a hospital or residential school.

In the World of the Out-of-Doors, demonstrate water safety for younger girls, help repair and maintain your council's small craft, help on a community clean water project.

If the project your group decides to undertake requires financial assistance in addition to your hard work, consider applying for a Reader's Digest Foundation Grant. If your project is accepted, the grant can help make your dream for your community come true. See the "Reader's Digest Foundation Grants" section for details.

You Decide Guide

After you have completed your community project for the final section of this Challenge, answer these questions. They will help you and your leader decide if you have satisfactorily completed the Challenge of Being a Girl Scout.

What have you discovered about Girl Scouting and how have you shared it with others?

What have I learned about myself? Where have I made improvements?

How have I shown that I can work with others in planning a project?

Why do I believe it is important for me to be a Girl Scout?

In what ways have I as a Girl Scout contributed to the well-being of my community?

Optional Ways to Earn the Challenge of Being a Girl Scout

If you choose, you may earn the American Indian Tradition Award, if you are of American Indian descent, or the religious recognition sponsored by your religious group as part of this Challenge. If you do this, it may be substituted for preps 2, 3, and 4. To earn the Challenge of Being a Girl Scout, prep 1, your option, and the Challenge must be completed.

Religious Recognitions

Through Girl Scouting, each girl is encouraged to become a stronger member of her own religious group. To help girls grow in this area, religious recognition programs have been developed and are handled by the religious groups themselves.

By working on a religious recognition as part of the Challenge, you will be doing more work than girls who earn the Challenge the traditional way. However, remember that you will receive two insignia: the Challenge pin and your religious recognition. They symbolize your commitment and your effort.

The religious recognition programs listed here are available nationwide. There are also many religious recognition programs, not nationally available, which have been developed by individual religious groups for local use. Check with your local clergy for information on such programs in your area.

For girls of the Roman Catholic faith:
The Marian Medal, a program for girls ages 12 through 15, involves participants in an understanding of Mary as a model of openness and spirituality, a woman of the church. For further information, talk to your parish priest or get in touch with your Roman Catholic Diocesan Youth Director or Girl Scout Chaplain.

For girls of the Jewish faith:
The Menorah Award, for girls ages 11 and older, emphasizes understanding of a girl's Jewish heritage through daily home observances, Sabbath and holiday observances, study of the Bible and Jewish history, and learning about the Jewish community in the United States and worldwide. For further information, a booklet outlining the requirements for the Menorah Award is available for a small fee from the National Jewish Girl Scout Committee, Synagogue Council of America, 10 East 40th Street, Suite 4210, New York, N.Y. 10016.

For girls of the Reorganized Church of Jesus Christ of the Latter Day Saints:
The Light of Life Award, for junior high girls, is a program to stimulate girls to think maturely about God, religion, and their church and to involve girls in meaningful Christian service.

The World Community series has three age-level programs that lead a girl through interesting growing experiences in all the important aspects of life:

Light of the World, for ages 8 through 10.

Liahona, for ages 11 through 14.

Exploring My Life and World, for ages 15 through 18.

A descriptive brochure on any program may be obtained by writing to the Christian Education Office, The Auditorium, P.O. Box 1059, Independence, Mo. 64051.

For girls of the Eastern Orthodox faith:

Alpha Omega, for girls ages 11 and older, emphasizes a girl's life and actions as an Orthodox Christian, the work and organization of her parish church, and service projects for the church. For further information, copies of the Alpha Omega Program Service Book are available for a small fee from the Orthodox Scouting Commission, 1345 Fairfield Woods Road, Fairfield, Conn. 06430.

For girls of the Protestant faith:

The God and Community Award, for girls ages 11 and older of the various Protestant denominations, is designed to help a girl in her spiritual growth through Bible study and prayer, learning about her own church, and giving service to the church.

This award was developed by Church Women United of Kansas City and is currently sponsored throughout the nation by various persons and organizations. For further information, the requirements are published in a Service Record Book, available for a small fee from Church Women United, God and Community Award, Box 17091, Kansas City, Mo. 64132.

The God and Country series, developed by the Church Commission for Civic Youth-Serving Agencies for young people of the Protestant faiths, has three units:

God and Family, for ages 9 and 10.

God and Church, for ages 11 through 14, provides a girl an opportunity to know her pastor and counselor better, to understand her church's structure and objectives, and to participate in services and projects that will give her a better understanding of the mission of her church.

God and Life, for ages 15 through 18, a program in which young adults, working with their pastor or counselor, will concern themselves with their faith and how they relate to their church, their family, their community, and their country.

For further information, a student workbook for the God and Church unit and the combined student workbook and counselor manual for the God and Life unit can be ordered for a small fee from Program of Religious Activity with Youth, Box 179, St. Louis, Mo. 63166.

For girls of the Lutheran faith:

God-Home-Country, for girls ages 12 and older, is designed to motivate girls to be active participants in all aspects of their church's program and to think deeply about participation in congregational and community life in response to God's love leading them to faith. For further information, write National Youth Agency Relationship, Lutheran Council in the U.S.A., 360 Park Avenue South, New York, N.Y. 10016.

For girls of the Buddhist faith:

The Padma Award, a four-part program with activities for Brownie, Junior, Cadette, and Senior Girl Scouts, is designed to help girls put into practice the ideals of the Buddhist faith and of the Girl Scout Promise and Law. A booklet about the Padma Award, describing its purpose and outlining the requirements, is available for a small fee from the Youth Department, Buddhist Churches of America, 1710 Octavia Street, San Francisco, Calif. 94109.

American Indian Tradition Award

Girl Scouts who are of American Indian descent are eligible to work toward the American Indian Tradition Award. This award was developed by the American Indian Seminar and may be counted toward part of the Challenge of Being a Girl Scout. It may be substituted for Challenge preps 2, 3, and 4.

Requirements for the American Indian Tradition Award are:

1. Be a registered Girl Scout, active in your troop.
2. Produce one item of the tribe's craftwork.
3. Make a tribal dress.
4. Be able to do two traditional dances.
5. Know two traditional songs.
6. Prepare two traditional foods.

Your Girl Scout leader should check that you have successfully fulfilled these requirements. The award will be presented at the American Indian Seminar, held annually by American Indian youth and their leaders who are active in Girl Scouting or Boy Scouting. Girl Scouts of American Indian origin who can meet the requirements of the American Indian Tradition Award but are unable to attend the seminar may receive the award from their tribal council. It has been customary for those earning the American Indian Tradition Award at the seminar to perform at least one of the dances and songs while wearing the dress made for the award.

The Challenge of Living the Promise and Law

Being able to explain the Girl Scout Promise and Law is one thing, but showing you have a true "working knowledge" of them in your daily life is another. As you do this Challenge, you will search your feelings and attitudes to discover whether the Promise and Law are really a part of you and guide you each day, now and in the future.

You do a community service project as the final part of this Challenge. The Challenge project you choose to do should be one that you feel is very important and that expresses your understanding of the ideals of Girl Scouting. Completing this Challenge says you care in so many ways.

This Challenge has five sections. To earn the Challenge of Living the Promise and Law, complete the first four sections before starting the last section. This section contains your Challenge to contribute to your community's well-being in a worthwhile project. You may work on all sections alone or with others who share your interest. The first four sections may be completed in any order. You may work on them one at a time or simultaneously. When you have completed them, you are ready to do the final Challenge project.

Together with your troop leader, you decide when you have satisfactorily completed each section of this Challenge. There are summaries after the first four sections and an evaluation guide to be used at the end of your Challenge project to help you do this.

Knowing About Girl Scouting

Take stock of your understanding of the Girl Scout Promise and Law by getting involved in Girl Scouting beyond your troop. The activity you select should not be something you have done or plan to do in order to fulfill the requirements of other recognitions. Figure on a minimum of eight hours of activity.

As you are serving as a Girl Scout volunteer, try to find out the following about the adult(s) you work with:

Why she/he volunteers.

What other voluntary commitments she/he has.

How her/his family responsibilities and paid employment (if any) relate to her/his volunteer work.

Here are some suggested activities:

Serve as a Girl Scout representative to a meeting sponsored by another organization.

Attend the National Council Session of GSUSA (if selected by your council).

Participate in a Girl Scout regional, national, or international wider opportunity.

Serve on a Cadette/Senior Planning Board or in a councilwide girl planning group.

Help plan a Cadette or Senior Girl Scout conference; Thinking Day event; or other special event in your council, neighborhood, or geographic service unit.

Serve on the council board or one of the committees in your council.

Participate in a council-sponsored training conference or event of Girl Scout volunteers.

Plan and carry out a project which will explain the origin, purpose, and use of the Juliette Low World Friendship Fund.

Conduct tours of council properties/facilities.

Provide home hospitality for Girl Guides or Girl Scouts from other countries or other parts of this country.

Participate in activities sponsored by Campus Girl Scouts.

Summarize your Girl Scout activities beyond the troop:

_____

_____

and some of what you learned about being a Girl Scout volunteer:

_____

_____

_____

Date: _____

Knowing Myself Better

Ask a friend your own age or older to discuss with you what she feels are your strengths and weaknesses. Compare what she tells you to your own image of yourself. Do the same activity with at least one adult. Once again, compare what you find out about yourself.

Design your own self-development plan for at least two months. Set some goals for yourself. Think about:

What do I want to do in the next six months, the next year?

What are my long-range goals for the next five years? ten years?

What do I want to start working on right now?

What are my leisure and employment plans for the future?

A goal might be to learn a skill, expand your ability to relate to others, practice budgeting, improve your figure, explore careers you are interested in, or anything that you feel will help you to develop your potentials. Write a contract with yourself, making sure to include your special goal, when you plan to reach it (how long), and how you're going to reach it (outline your plan). Write out the details of your agreement with yourself. Sign and date it. Refer to your contract once a week to help you keep your commitment to yourself.

Summarize your goal: _____

_____.

the progress you've made toward it: _____

_____.

how you may continue your goal or focus, or another goal, in weeks to come:

_____

_____

Date: _____

Me and Others Profile

	adult family members	sister/brother	close friend	females my age	older females (neighbors/employers/ teachers)	males my age	older males (neighbors/employers/ teachers)	people from racial, ethnic, religious groups not my	children
I am able to:									
Show respect for ideas and opinions of									
Trust									
Share my ideas and opinions with									
Consider the feelings of									
Be understanding of actions contrary to my values and beliefs of									
Give assistance when problems, physical, mental, or emotional, seem difficult for									
Work cooperatively to do a job or project with									
Ask for the help of									
Make new friends with									
Share my skills and talents with									
Make choices based upon the Girl Scout Promise and Law that differ from opinion of									
Take a leadership role with									
Explain my point of view to									

Relating to Others

Fill in the "Me and Others Profile" to examine your skills in relating to others. Based on your answers, plan to increase your skills in at least one area of relating. Set a goal for yourself and work on it for a minimum of two months. Keep the profile to refer to from time to time.

Summarize your plan to increase your skills in relating to others:

_____

_____.

and something you learned about yourself in filling out the "Me and Others Profile":

_____

_____

Date: _____

Developing Values for Living

Keep a journal for a minimum of two months on where you stand on your values. Make entries two or three times a week. Keep notes on how you live up to the Girl Scout Promise and each part of the Girl Scout Law.

Some things you might include are:

action(s) that show you understand what the Promise or a part of the Law means in your daily life,

how you have used ideas in the Promise and Law to help or seek help for a friend or acquaintance who has a problem related to family relationships, schoolwork, alcoholism, relationships with peers, drugs, physical or mental abuse, etc.,

what ways your actions/thinking were influenced (positively or negatively) by some other person(s),

what ways you have acted on the Promise or part of the Law repeatedly and how it has become a part of your daily living.

Summarize your journal notes of discoveries about yourself and your values:

_____

_____.

and something you've done you are really proud of:

_____

_____

_____.

Think about this question: Did you find that what you actually say and do, matches what you say you believe?

Date: _____

The Challenge

As a Girl Scout, you have probably been involved in many projects that contribute to your community's well-being. To complete this section of the Challenge of Living the Promise and Law, you must design, develop, and carry out a project that will benefit your community in some way. The project you select will show others what you value. Your Challenge project should be in an area you care about deeply. Choose something you feel you will continue to be concerned about and involved with in some way for several years after you complete your Challenge projects and receive your Challenge insignia. You may choose to work on this section alone or with others. Just be sure that you work on something you personally feel is important.

You may choose to complete a volunteer service bar to fulfill this part of the Challenge as described above. If you have completed a volunteer service bar previously, you may complete a second volunteer service bar in the same area or complete a new volunteer service bar in another area or world of interest. If you complete a volunteer service bar for this Challenge, you must also decide on how you plan to continue your involvement in the future and complete the following evaluation. (See the "Volunteer Service" chapter for full details about volunteer service projects.)

You may wish to refer to the chapter entitled "Community Service" for help in getting started. Remember that you need to decide on how you could continue your interest and involvement in the goals of your Challenge project. You are making a commitment to do something now, as well as in the future. The essential ingredient is that you are committed to doing something, even though the details of how and when may change.

After you have completed your Challenge project, use the evaluation guide below to help you and your leader decide if you have satisfactorily completed the Challenge of Living the Promise and Law.

What have I discovered about the work of Girl Scouting and about at least one staff or volunteer position?

In what situations have I demonstrated a real understanding of the Promise and Law by applying them to everyday living?

In what ways have I shown that I am capable of working, planning, and sharing with a group?

How have I shown through action and attitude my personal integrity and honor?

How has my project benefited others?

In what ways could I continue my interest in this area I value over the next several years? What do I hope to do right away?

Pencil Drawing, William De Mott, age 17, Newark, N.Y.

EXPLORE THE WORLDS OF INTEREST

How can you manage to do all the things you want to do? Discover ideas you have never thought of before? Meet people with whom you share a special interest?

One way might be to do some of the activities in one of the five interest projects found in this book. In *Let's Make It Happen!,* you will find 22 other interest projects as well as information about writing your own. Each interest project offers you a choice of 12 activities and suggests people and groups who might help you. To earn an interest project certificate and the privilege of wearing the patch, you need to complete eight of the 12 activities listed.

The interest projects in this book are called dabblers. These sampler-type activities will help you to get acquainted with the many possibilities in a particular world of interest. Here's what the worlds of interest are:

The World of Well-Being. Here the focus is on physical and emotional health, nutrition, and exercise. Develop your skills in interpersonal relationships. Learn about the home, safety, work, leisure, and consumer awareness.

The World of People. Explore the various cultures in American society and around the world. Build pride in your heritage, while appreciating and respecting those of others.

The World of Today and Tomorrow. Discover the how and why of things, exploring and experimenting with the many technologies that touch daily life. Learn to deal with change, and look to future events, roles, and responsibilities with enthusiasm.

The World of the Arts. Involve yourself in the whole range of arts—visual, performing, and literary. Enjoy and express yourself through various art forms and appreciate the artistic talents and contributions of others.

The World of the Out-of-Doors. Enjoy and appreciate the out-of-doors. Live in and care for the natural environment, and understand and respect the interdependence of all living things.

After each world's dabbler interest project, you will find a resource list that can start you on your way. Your town or school library may have a whole range of materials on the subject you are working on, so don't limit yourself to just those listed. Look around you and discover local resources that can help you complete the interest project.

If you are ready to expand on a dabbler project by writing your own interest project, you might try to design one using the guidelines in *Let's Make It Happen!,* on page 69. Use the suggested resources to give you ideas for other activities too.

When you complete eight or more activities in an interest project, you earn an interest project recognition certificate and the right to wear that interest project patch. This is so whether you do one of the dabbler interest projects in this book, a project from *Let's Make It Happen!,* or one you have written for yourself or your group. Your leader will have information about your council's plan for making these recognitions available.

Before you begin any interest project, review the introductory material in *Let's Make It Happen!,* pages 4–10, 69–72. These sections will help you understand how to carry out a project. Remember, you will need to decide right from the start which activities you would like to do, and which alternates within each activity.

Create Your Own World of Well-Being

What do I plan to do with my life? How do I get where I want to go? What do I value most in life? What decisions do I have to make? Perhaps these are questions you have asked yourself or will ask in the near future. Exploring the World of Well-Being will help you discover answers to these questions, plus more.

Planning a positive path to get where you want to go begins with getting to know the most important person in your life — you. Knowing yourself, your strengths, weaknesses, interests, values, needs, and emotions is all a part of your being. To know how to take care of your body, make decisions, solve problems, cope with feelings, relate to others, and develop a knowledge of health and safety are essential ingredients of your total makeup. Knowing yourself doesn't stop with an interest project, it is a lifelong process.

The World of Well-Being deals with the way you think, feel, and act. Interesting thoughts and ideas, shared and expressed feelings, and successful and enjoyable actions, describe the exciting opportunities awaiting you in the World of Well-Being.

In the pages that follow and in the years ahead, you will continue to learn more about yourself. The knowledge you gain from looking closely at yourself, combined with the experiences you gain from the World of Well-Being, will give you the power to plan positive experiences, and to set and achieve realistic goals for yourself. Remember, a safe, healthy, and happy future lies within you.

Here are 12 ways to find out how much the World of Well-Being affects your life. Do eight or more activities to earn a recognition certificate for this dabbler interest project.

BEAUTY IS... Plan and conduct a beauty workshop. Invite consultants to talk with you about, or demonstrate solutions to, some of your concerns, such as skin, hair, makeup, teeth, dieting, and shaping up. Consultants might include a cosmetologist, dermatologist, beautician, dentist, physician, or physical education teacher.

NUTRITIOUS EATING. Create and present an action game or visual presentation (puppet show, skit, display) to help younger children understand the importance of good nutrition. You might include proper eating habits, basic food groups, required nutrients, snack foods, and body weight.

FEELINGS. List all the feelings you have experienced in the past week. Write down whether each feeling was positive, negative, or neutral. Have other members of your group do the same thing. Compare your feelings (and their origins) with those of the other people. Identify the five most common positive feelings and the five most common negative feelings. Discuss ways to manage your negative feelings. Analyze what situations contributed to your positive feelings.

BE PREPARED! Did you know that auto accidents are the leading cause of death between ages 15 and 24? Survey at least five friends to find out if they, or someone close to them, have been in an auto accident in the past year. Identify where and why the accident occurred and the safety measures that can be taken to protect youth and other drivers on the road.

GROWING UP. Plan an event such as a workshop, clinic, or demonstration to help you, your friends, parents, and others find answers to the many concerns teenagers have about adolescence. For example, relationships with boys; relationships with adults; the effects of smoking, drinking, and taking drugs; emotional and body changes; etc. Ask parents, clergy, teachers, physicians, and other adults to assist you in planning this event. Books, magazines, and local or national organizations may also be helpful, reliable resources. Evaluate your plan along the way and at the end of the event.

DO IT THE INTERNATIONAL WAY. Prepare a well-balanced international meal at home or on the trail for family or friends. Decide what you will serve and the type of entertainment to accompany the meal. Make arrangements for buying the ingredients, preparing the food, serving, and cleaning up. Add the recipes to your recipe file.

LEND A HELPING HAND. Volunteer to assist in a nursery school, day-care center, day camp, playground, health or community center for at least ten hours. First, observe the children, teens, or adults you will be working with. Then, help plan fun activities which are suitable for them.

IMPROVE YOUR SKILLS. Demonstrate your ability to perform first aid skills by doing one or more of the following:

Assist a first aider for at least three troop meetings, a camp weekend trip, a blood donor drive, or at least two school or community sporting events.

OR

Prepare and teach at least two lessons on first aid skills, such as how to treat bleeding, burns, choking, poisoning, or how to give mouth-to-mouth resuscitation, at a school, a religious or community group meeting.

OR

Create a play, slide show, or charts that provide helpful first aid information to a school, religious or community group.

A SPORTING EVENT. Participate in one of the following events: a mini or Special Olympics, bike-a-thon, walk-a-thon, tournament, sports day, or New Games festival. Be sure you are physically prepared to participate in the event you select. A medical history and health examination are required for contact sports, a medical history for non-contact sports. See *Safety-Wise,* page 4.

OR

Find out how one of these events is organized and, with the help of your troop, plan to hold one. Recruit all the necessary people, such as players, coaches, officials, scorers, timers, equipment managers. Select a safe place to carry out the event. Evaluate your plan along the way and at the end of the event.

CONSUMER-WISE. Jot down at least five things you and your friends like to spend money on. Go comparison shopping and compare the cost, quality, care, and/or safety of these items. Then, design a booklet that gives teens tips on how to get the best buys for their money. You might include what to consider when purchasing these items, where and when to shop, fads, and advertising. Share this booklet with others.

A FAMILY AFFAIR. With a group of family members or friends, brainstorm the various problems that occur within families, such as the effects of a natural disaster, a death, frequent fighting, a runaway, drinking or drug problems, etc. Discuss or role play the different ways families can handle such problems to prevent being overwhelmed by them.

USE IT/WASTE IT. Keep an accurate record of all the things you do and the time you spend doing them for four to seven days. Include activities such as attending school, doing homework, watching television, reading, helping at home, working, traveling, dressing, eating, sleeping, visiting friends or relatives. At the end of the days, calculate the number of hours you spent on each activity. Make an advance weekly schedule that includes a hobby or leisure time activity you have been wanting to do, but couldn't seem to find the time for. Decide how much time you will spend doing it. Try out your schedule. Revise it until it fits *you.*

Where Do You Go from Here?

If you have enjoyed doing the activities in the World of Well-Being and wish to continue planning exciting experiences, there are many things you can do. For example, if your group would like to sponsor a citywide softball tournament, find a consultant who can help you develop a plan to learn the skills you need to organize the games and the event. The consultant could also take you one step further by helping you write your own interest project on softball. (See *Let's Make It Happen!,* page 69.) You can also find helpful suggestions in *Girl Scout Badges and Signs.*

Resources

Consultants: autoshop teacher, beautician, clergyperson, cooking instructor, cosmetologist, dentist, dermatologist, exercise instructor, first aid instructor, nurse, nutritionist, parents, park and recreation specialist, physical education teacher, physician, psychologist, public health worker.

National Organizations: get in touch with your local chapter first, or write to the national address given here.

American Alliance for Health, Physical Education, Recreation and Dance (AAHPERD)
1900 Association Drive
Reston, Va. 22091

American Medical Association
535 North Dearborn Street
Chicago, Ill. 60610

Consumer Product Safety Commission
1111 18th Street, N.W.
Washington, D.C. 20207

Special Olympics, Inc.
Suite 203
1701 K Street, N.W.
Washington, D.C. 20006

U.S. Department of Health and Human Services
Public Health Service
Alcohol, Drug Abuse and Mental Health Administration
5600 Fishers Lane
Rockville, Md. 20852

Girl Scout Resources

Games for Girl Scouts. Cat. No. 20–630, (rev. ed.) 1969.

Happily Appley: A Leader's Guide to Food Fun with Young Children. Cat. No. 19–995, 1975.

Safety-Wise. Cat. No. 26–205, 1977.

Books

American Red Cross. *Family Health and Home Nursing.* Garden City, N.Y.: Doubleday & Co., 1979.

———. *Standard First Aid and Personal Safety.* Garden City, N.Y.: Doubleday & Co., 1973.

Channing L. Bete Co. offers booklets for a small fee on health and safety topics, such as personal health care, mental health, alcohol and drugs, recreation, and highway safety. Available from Channing L. Bete Co., Inc., 200 State Road, South Deerfield, Mass. 01373.

New Games Foundation. *The New Games Book.* Garden City, N.Y.: Doubleday & Co., 1976.

Organizing Playdays and Large Group Activities, Rules for Co-Educational Activities and Sports, 1979. Available from AAHPERD Publications, P.O. Box 704, 44 Industrial Park Circle, Waldorf, Md. 20601.

Find Your Place in the World of People

What do backpacking along a trail with your troop, participating in an international wider opportunity, earning money for a family whose home was destroyed by fire, and coming to an agreement with your parents about dating, have in common? Each of these activities depends upon your involvement with other people. Anytime you learn more about another person, and put that learning into action, you are exploring the World of People. Each person in the world is special and all have many things in common. Everyone needs to be loved and to have friends. Everyone needs adequate food, clothing, and shelter. And everyone needs opportunities to learn and to express themselves. People have some differences, too. Some of these differences are individual, because each person is unique (there is no one else like *me*), and some differences are because everyone has a different heritage.

In today's world, people are all very dependent upon other people. The world works best when people can cooperate. Getting along with others means learning to share, to see things from other people's viewpoint, and to cooperate together to get things done.

When you read the newspaper or watch the evening news, do you ever wonder what you could do to help? What is your responsibility to the people of the world? or even to those in your community? No one has all the answers, but the more information you have, the more likely you are to make a wise decision. And decision-making is part of taking your place in the future.

Service is a way of relating your experiences and knowledge to the needs of others. It is not merely doing something for someone, but helping when and where you are needed. Whether it is in the troop, council, community, country, or world, service has been an important part of Girl Scouting for over 65 years.

Girl Scouting and Group Management

Photograph, Harry Fisher, age 17, Reseda, Calif.

A-1

Girl Scouting began because teenagers like yourself wanted it and made it happen. Girls wanted the fun and adventure that Girl Scouting offered and were eager to join the movement. Juliette Gordon Low, one of the primary forces of the Girl Guiding movement in England, had the determination and interest to bring Girl Scouting to girls and women in the United States.

Within two years after Girl Guiding began in England and Scotland, Juliette Low called the first meeting in Savannah, Georgia. On March 12, 1912, eighteen girls met with Mrs. Low and two other women to form the first two Girl Scout patrols.

In 1912 girls and women were discouraged from seeking any life or exploring any potential other than domestic interest. Juliette Low believed very strongly in an organization that would provide an opportunity for all girls to develop their full potential as creative, knowledgeable, capable women. She was a woman of action who never lost confidence in her special project.

Girl Scouting was such an innovation that the excitement it generated quickly spread throughout the country. Requests came in from all over asking how others could join. The movement grew, just as Juliette Low knew it would. Through succeeding decades, Girl Scouting has helped many girls and women in all parts of the United States gain more freedom and has widened their career opportunities.

Robert, Lord Baden-Powell,
the founder of Boy Scouting

Juliette Gordon Low

Juliette Gordon Low, whose nickname was Daisy, was a woman ahead of her time. Her skills and accomplishments have inspired several generations of girls and women. A world traveller and a skilled artist, she disregarded the limits on women of her time by extending her skills to sculpture and ironwork. But it was her vision for girls that was to become her life's work.

Daisy was a dedicated woman who did not let her deafness stand in her way. She was a leader, able to rally people from all levels of society to help her in making Girl Scouting possible. Her determination saw her through many

obstacles. Once she even sold her jewelry to help finance the development of the Girl Scouts as a national organization. Her goal realized, she never stopped expanding what Girl Scouting could offer.

Juliette Low's contributions to helping girls acquire skills and experience to take their part as leaders in today's world have been widely recognized. In 1948, the United States government issued a commemorative postage stamp in her honor. Her portrait hangs in the National Portrait Gallery in Washington, D.C., and a portrait bust is in the Hall of Fame of the State of Georgia.

Your Place in Girl Scouting

The great things you do in Girl Scouting, the fun and friendship you find, can all continue beyond your Cadette and Senior years right into adult Girl Scouting. There are many good reasons to remain part of the organization for your whole life. You can:

Pass on your skills and your caring ways to others.

Provide for tomorrow's girls what others have helped make possible for you.

Share a new closeness with other adults.

Continue to grow and develop through training opportunities and participation in exciting events and programs.

Make Girl Scouting everything you know it can be.

Be part of the continuation of something you care about — and something that cares for the todays and tomorrows of all girls and women.

Try out new volunteer and career responsibilities in an atmosphere that supports your development.

Be like the adults you admired as a girl member.

Moving into adult Girl Scouting opens a world of possibilities for you.

If you are enrolled at a college or university, Campus Girl Scouts will give you the opportunity to meet college students and work with Girl Scouting in your college community. If you are working in a community where a Campus Girl Scout chapter has been formed, you may join the collegians and continue your Girl Scout activities with them.

Your Girl Scout council welcomes your membership. There are many opportunities you can fill that will call for your talents and energies. To give you an idea of the scope of your possibilities, here are a few. You'll see that they require different time commitments/different skills.

Serve as a program consultant or a council trainer.

Accompany troops on trips or camping events.

Work on a fund-raising drive.

Write about Girl Scouting in the council bulletin.

Participate in a wider opportunity designed for adults.

Help with special events or work on a selection committee for wider opportunities.

Serve as a troop leader.

Be a member of a service team — as a troop organizer or consultant, as a neighborhood chairman.

Serve as a delegate to the National Council Session, if elected.

Serve on the council's board of directors or council board committees.

Work as an employed staff member of your council — perhaps as a field adviser, camp director, program or training director, or as executive director.

Just as there are adult responsibilities/opportunities within your council, the national organization has similar responsibilities. The National Board of Directors is composed of dedicated volunteers who make decisions on the policies the organization should follow.

The Girl Scout organization also needs executive staff to carry out the directions of the National Board and its committees. Staff employed in Girl Scouting have a wide choice of jobs in locations around the country and even abroad. There are opportunities for people knowledgeable in program, training, fund development, human relations and personnel, sales, membership, management, and council operations.

Whatever your interests are, take the time now to investigate the possibilities open to you. That way, you will have the knowledge and training necessary to move into adult Girl Scouting with ease.

The Girl Scout Organization

If you were to ask for a technical explanation of a Girl Scout council, you would find out that it is a corporation responsible for Girl Scout operations within a defined jurisdiction. What does this mean? It means that your council makes Girl Scouting happen in your area. Your council is people, both volunteers and employed staff, who carry out the business of Girl Scouting. There are more than 300 Girl Scout councils in the United States today.

Through Girl Scout councils, Girl Scout camps are owned and operated, leaders trained, and a great variety of events and workshops planned and presented. Your council is always developing Girl Scout opportunities for you to take advantage of. Because the council is there to help and provide services to you and to the Girl Scout adults who work with you, you will see references to "your council" or "your council office" throughout this book.

Possibly you could serve on planning boards or task groups in your council and thus bring your ideas and input into the workings of Girl Scouting. Your council bylaws may provide a chance for you to be elected to your council's board or to be a council representative at the National Council Session.

Girl Scouts of the United States of America (GSUSA) is a corporation chartered by Congress. Members of the National Council, who are elected representatives of Girl Scout councils, meet in convention every three years to set directions for Girl Scouting throughout the United States. Since girls are as much a part of the movement as adults, members of the National Council can be as young as 14 years of age. That might mean you!

The National Council is also responsible for electing the National Board of Directors and for making any changes in the Girl Scout constitution.

Through its National Board of Directors and its employed staff, Girl Scouts of the U.S.A. provides services both to Girl Scout councils across the country and to individual members like you. Training events for national volunteers and for council administrative staff, the operation of the national centers, the publication of handbooks such as *You Make the Difference,* and the mailing of *Runways* directly to you are all examples of some of these services. Did you realize that membership dues are one of the main sources of income for GSUSA?

The Girl Scout National Centers

Three Girl Scout national centers can help widen the opportunities that Girl Scouting offers to you. Owned and operated by Girl Scouts of the U.S.A., these centers exist for you — your membership dues help to keep them open.

What do these centers mean to you? If you go to one of your national centers, you will have a chance to meet Girl Scouts from across the country. Together, you can participate in activities as different as the settings of each of these centers. The national centers offer you a chance to be on your own, traveling and exploring new worlds and adventures.

National Center West, 15,000 acres of rugged wilderness located in Wyoming, offers a taste of the West. Picture yourself riding a horse across the vast mesas, backpacking down a canyon pass, stalking wildlife with your camera, or primitive camping, and you'll have some idea of the adventures awaiting you at this center.

The Juliette Gordon Low Girl Scout National Center has a very different perspective. In the heart of downtown Savannah, Georgia, the center is part of the largest National Historic Landmark District in the United States. Here, at the only national Girl Scout public museum, you can explore the early Americana of Daisy Low's childhood. You can visit her home, tour this seaport city, and experience the past and present of our country's South.

Edith Macy Girl Scout National Center is situated just 35 miles from the middle of New York City. The variety of activities that can originate at Macy is terrific and program events staged here are just beginning to tap the full potential of the area. Your explorations can range from walks down city streets by the United Nations to hikes along American Indian trails and inland marshes near the historic Hudson River.

Both Macy and National Center West offer you an extra bonus. They have the facilities to serve as hostels for traveling Girl Scout troops.

If you have been tempted by these brief descriptions and want to know more, write to the following addresses:

Juliette Gordon Low Girl Scout National Center
142 Bull Street
Savannah, Georgia 31401

Edith Macy Girl Scout National Center
c/o Girl Scouts of the U.S.A.
830 Third Avenue
New York, N.Y. 10022

Girl Scout National Center West
Box 95
Ten Sleep, Wyoming 82442

Wider Opportunities

A wider opportunity is exactly what you would expect from its name. It is your opportunity to meet people, discover new places, try your hand at different skills, and even travel to distant states or foreign countries. A wider opportunity is any Girl Scout activity that takes you outside your own troop and council or, if your council is the sponsor, an event that brings Girl Scouts from other areas to you. The program, activities, and participants can vary greatly, but a wider opportunity always extends your range beyond the circle of your troop.

These opportunities are open to you and other Girl Scouts on a regional or nationwide basis and their purpose is to broaden your horizons and challenge your independence. You could find yourself camping under desert skies with dozens of other troops, sailing the coast with Girl Scouts from across the country, or journeying to another country.

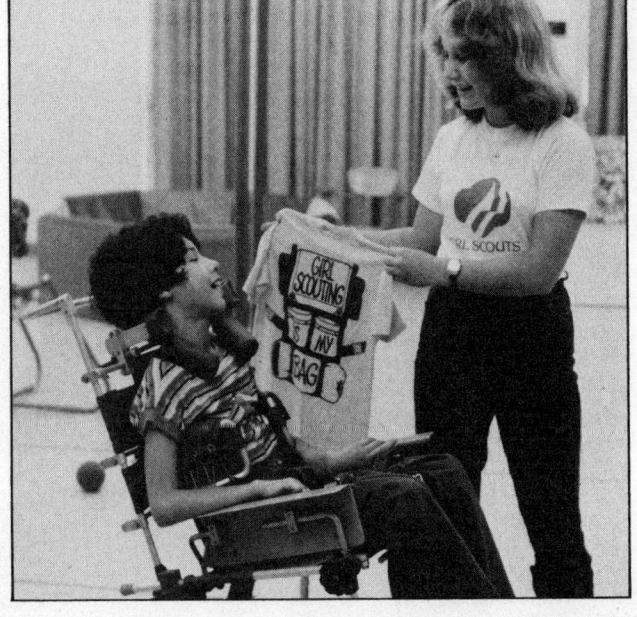

A wider opportunity can be:

planned for and by one troop/group, such as a three-day or longer trip

organized for two to 50 or even more troops or patrols on a service area, district, or councilwide basis

designed for 10–1,000 or more individuals on a neighborhood, district, councilwide, intercouncil, or national basis

international in scope

Most wider opportunities are offered right in your own backyard — by your own council or a neighboring council. Ask your leader about the possibilities for participating in both summer and winter council events.

As a registered Cadette or Senior Girl Scout, you will receive a copy of *Runways,* an annual publication of Girl Scouts of the U.S.A. It describes national and international wider opportunities offered by councils across the country and by Girl Scouts of the U.S.A. In it you will find important information, including dates, cost, special requirements and, of course, a description of what you will do. Each issue of *Runways* gives you step-by-step instructions for applying for the wider opportunities offered that year. You may also be eligible for additional wider opportunities not included in *Runways.* Councils and Girl Scouts of the U.S.A. often sponsor events that are only open to Girl Scouts in a particular region or that were prepared after *Runways'* publication, so be alert for any announcements regarding these.

Runways will provide you with advice on how to present your application request to your best advantage. These instructions will also help you apply for opportunities not offered in *Runways.* You can get further helpful sugges-

tions and information from your leader, council, or other Girl Scouts familiar with the process.

Financial assistance is sometimes available for particular events. Girls chosen for international opportunities through Girl Scouts of the U.S.A. will have part of their expenses paid by the Juliette Low World Friendship Fund. The DeWitt Wallace Reader's Digest Scholarship Fund provides assistance to some patrols selected for the Wyoming Trek (Girl Scout groups who plan and carry out their own trip to National Center West). Troop money-earning activities are also possible, so keep this in mind. Your council will be able to direct you in your efforts for financing your opportunity.

If you have been selected for an event, know what lies ahead for you. Background information will help you gain the most from your experience. A good source of instructions on travel readiness is *Planning Trips With Girl Scouts* (GSUSA, Cat. No. 19–998, 1977).

Internationally Speaking

How many Girl Scouts do you know or have you met? If you're fairly new to Girl Scouting, you may know only your own group. If you've been a member for a while you may know a dozen, fifty, or a few hundred Girl Scouts. If you've been on a wider opportunity to another state or country, you've met quite a few — maybe more than a thousand. One thing is certain, you're not alone.

Did you know:

You have about eight million sisters in approximately 100 countries.

You are part of the largest international organization for girls and women in the world.

Representatives of this organization meet often with officials at the United Nations.

Some of the most influential women in the world today are members of Girl Scouts.

You have a rich and proud heritage as a Girl Scout.

No matter what their language, all members of Girl Scouting and Girl Guiding share adherence to the same basic principles of a Promise and Law. In each country where the movement is represented, it must be free from political control and open to all girls, without regard to race, color, religion, or any other circumstances.

The World Association

National organizations may be elected to membership in the World Association of Girl Guides and Girl Scouts (WAGGGS for short). Every three years, representatives of these national organizations meet together at a world conference to discuss and vote on matters of common interest to Girl Guides and Girl Scouts everywhere. Between world conferences, the business of the World Association is carried on by international committees of volunteers and by international staff at the World Bureau in London, England.

In most countries, there is one Girl Guide/Girl Scout organization with membership open to all girls. However, in some countries, mainly in Europe where the tradition of a state church persists, there may be several separate Girl Guide associations — one affiliated with the state church and others completely separate. They generally have different uniforms. Where this pattern exists, the various Girl Guide associations are federated into one single representative organization for the world conference, so that no country has more than one vote. In many countries, the original traditions established by Lord Baden-Powell are still strictly adhered to. Girl Guides regularly use the Girl Guide salute and handshake, and practice traditional ceremonies, especially when raising or lowering the flag. And then, of course, there's the most obvious difference of all — most Girl Guides wear blue, not green, uniforms.

The World Centers

Girl Scouts everywhere who are 14 or older may stay at the world centers which are owned and operated by WAGGGS. For information on how, contact your council office. The world centers are:

Our Chalet, Adelboden, Switzerland — founded 1932, a gift of Blanche Storrow, of Boston, Mass. This center, high in the Swiss Alps, focuses on the out-of-doors — hiking and mountain-climbing in the summer months, skiing in the winter.

Olave House, London, England — founded 1939. Located in the heart of London, this center serves as a hostel for Girl Scout travelers and provides the perfect base from which to explore London and southern England. Known as Our Ark, the center was re-named Olave House in 1963, honoring Olave, Lady Baden-Powell.

Our Cabaña, Cuernavaca, Mexico — founded 1957. Here, surrounded by bright tropical flowers, Girl Guides and Girl Scouts learn and practice Mexican crafts and customs and participate in community service projects.

Sangam, Poona, India — founded 1966. Sangam, a Sanskrit word meaning "coming together," literally describes what happens at this beautiful program center, where girls of Eastern and Western cultures have a chance to meet and share their heritages, and to work together in community service.

Program 'Round the World

If you visit a world center, or perhaps go on an international wider opportunity, you may find yourself observing many differences and similarities in the way other Girl Guides and Girl Scouts do things. It is true that we all have a Promise and Law, share the same traditions, and may even sing the same songs; yet in other countries the main program activities may be quite different from ours.

In the Scandinavian countries, where the government provides all or most necessary services, there is much less attention on service work, unlike our Latin American friends who have a strong service program. Northern European program is focused almost entirely on the out-of-doors; girls learn very advanced camping and outdoor survival skills. In contrast, environmental conditions in Latin America make camping difficult or not entirely safe. For these girls, camping is just beginning to become a significant part of the Girl Guiding program.

In some industrialized countries, a major element of the Girl Guide program is career exploration, including those careers that were once considered for "men only." A program of this type is also providing opportunities in many developing countries of Africa and Asia. Here, where women have been traditionally kept out of the market economy and denied avenues of influence, Girl Guiding offers the chance to prove their worth and to learn valuable skills.

Whatever the country, the Girl Guide or Girl Scout program answers the needs of young women who are striving to reach their fullest potential in the growing world of which they are a part.

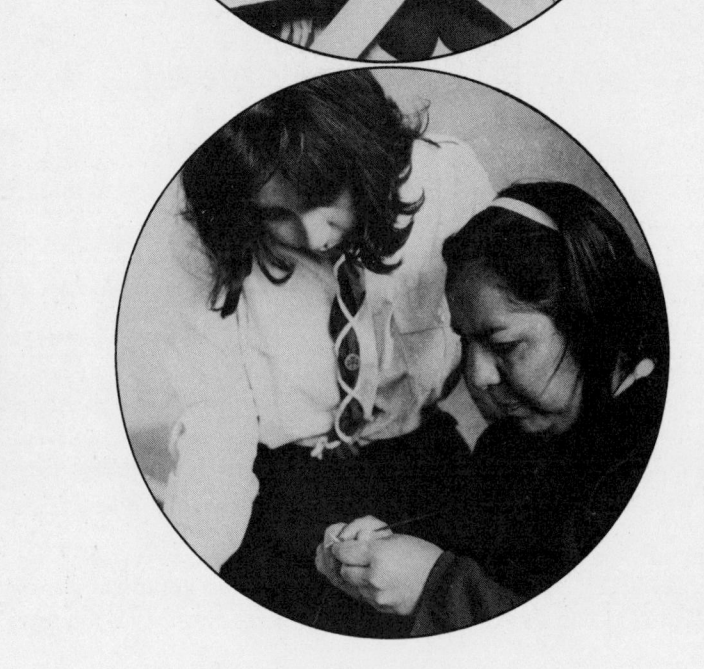

Thinking Day

You are one of approximately eight million girls and women who, each in her own way, cares about the heritage we all share in Girl Guiding/Girl Scouting. One common tradition is called Thinking Day — February 22. The birthday of the founder of Boy Scouting, Lord Baden-Powell, and of the World Chief Guide, Lady Baden-Powell, February 22 is the day for Girl Guides and Girl Scouts everywhere to think about their sisters around the world. Most troops plan something very special for that day; included in the ceremonies is an opportunity to contribute to the Juliette Low World Friendship Fund.

In the United States, the Juliette Low World Friendship Fund (JLWFF) was set up in 1927, several years before the World Association established the Thinking Day Fund in 1932. Because the latter helps make it possible for Girl Guiding to keep growing, each year part of the contributions to the Juliette Low World Friendship Fund are sent to the Thinking Day Fund. In this way, you and all other Girl Scouts have a tangible way of reaching out in love to the other members of your worldwide family.

These voluntary contributions from members around the world are used to help Girl Guides in developing countries by giving financial support to Girl Guide projects that fight illiteracy and malnutrition and that aid the handicapped and those in need of basic health care. Through the Thinking Day Fund, Girl Guide handbooks are printed and distributed to girls who would otherwise never see a handbook and know about Girl Guiding. Trainers are sent to help women in remote communities learn how to set up Girl Guiding and help it meet their needs. Without the Thinking Day Fund, your worldwide family would not be nearly as large, diverse, and healthy as it is today.

Highlights of Girl Scout History 1910–1980

1910
Girl Guide movement begins in England.

1912
Juliette Gordon Low brings Girl Guiding to the U.S.A.
First troop of 18 teens meets March 12 in Savannah, Georgia. Uniforms, dark blue.

1913
Girl Scouts becomes new name for Girl Guides in the U.S.A.

First Girl Scout handbook issued —*How Girls Can Help Their Country*.

1914
Trefoil design becomes sign of membership.

1916
First Brownie-age troop organized in Marblehead, Massachusetts.

1917
First troop of physically handicapped girls in the United States organized in New York City.

1926
Site of Edith Macy Girl Scout National Center given to Girl Scouts. First international conferences held there with representatives from 29 countries.

1927
First group of U.S. Girl Scouts goes to international event in Switzerland.

Juliette Low World Friendship Fund started.

First registration of United States Girl Scout Troops on Foreign Soil (TOFS).

1929
Our Chalet given to World Association of Girl Guides and Girl Scouts by Mrs. James J. Storrow of Boston.

1930
First recorded all-American Indian Girl Scout troop in Pawnee, Oklahoma.

1932
World Flag, designed by Norwegian Girl Guide, adopted.

March 12 becomes official birthday of Girl Scouts.

1933
First all-American Indian Girl Scout camp and conference in Anadarko, Oklahoma.

1935
Conference of leaders of handicapped Girl Scouts held in New York City.

1936
First nationally franchised Girl Scout cookie sale.

1937
First international meeting of teen Girl Guides and Girl Scouts held in U.S.A.

1938
First Senior Girl Scout encampment. Teens from 32 states attend at Camp Cloud Rim, Utah.

1940
First Girl Scout troops from institutions for mentally and socially handicapped people are registered.

1944
Girl Scouts register one million members.

1947
Senior Girl Scouts attend National Council Session for first time.

Name change for organization — from Girl Scouts to Girl Scouts of the United States of America.

1948
Juliette Low postage stamp issued.

1950
Girl Scouts of the U.S.A. is given Congressional Charter.

1953
Our Cabaña in Cuernavaca, Mexico, is acquired by WAGGGS.

Juliette Gordon Low Birthplace purchased by Girl Scouts of the U.S.A.

1962

Fiftieth anniversary. Post Office issues commemorative Girl Scout stamp.

1963

New program format developed; four age levels established.

1964

Girl Scout handbooks issued in Braille.

1965

Brownie handbook published in Spanish.

1966

Juliette Gordon Low Birthplace becomes National Historic Landmark.

1968

Girl Scout National Center West established.

Campus Girl Scouts officially recognized.

1969

416 teens from 39 states attend All-States Rendezvous at Girl Scout National Center West.

1970

Conference on Scouting for Black Girls held in Atlanta.

30 millionth member of GSUSA is registered.

1971

First national conference on Girl Scouting — Mexican-American Style held at Prescott, Arizona.

1972

New wording for the Girl Scout Promise and Law adopted.

National Council lowers age limit of National Council members to 14.

1973

Membership extended to six-year-olds through revision in membership standards.

Juliette Gordon Low portrait presented by GSUSA to National Portrait Gallery of Smithsonian Institution.

1974

Juliette Gordon Low bust placed in Georgia's Hall of Fame.

1977

Worlds to Explore: Handbook for Brownie and Junior Girl Scouts published; program activities arranged into five worlds of interest.

1978

New Girl Scout emblem launched, features three-profile silhouette of girls' faces.

From Dreams to Reality: Adventures in Careers issued, first part of the new program for Cadette and Senior Girl Scouts.

1979

Let's Make It Happen! issued, second part of the new program for Cadette and Senior Girl Scouts.

1980

You Make the Difference: The Handbook for Cadette and Senior Girl Scouts issued, completing the new program for teens.

New recognition system for Girl Scouts; highest award, the Girl Scout Gold Award, established.

Getting Together, or How to Work in Groups

"Welcome aboard!"
"Let's get together!"
"Join us!"

Such warm invitations can make you feel good right away and put you in the mood to enjoy being with others in a group. Although being a Girl Scout is very personal, you aren't left to do it alone. Girl Scouting is designed for you to meet people, make friends, and work together with them in groups. This means getting together and having the opportunity for each of you to reach your own goals and contribute to the goals of your group as well.

And that's what this part of the book is all about: working in groups. After you've been through this section, you'll have more than a formula for group success — you'll know the elements and will be able to select the ones you want for yourself. You can decide what parts go together, how to mix them, and when your efforts are done to suit you. You'll see that there's no one "right" way, no single "best"

choice for group action. In Girl Scout groups, the measure of "right" and "best" is the Girl Scout Promise and Law. You'll discover its basics are part of any group that's effective and efficient.

Let's turn the spotlight on the best thing about groups: the people whose lives are touched by your group (including you!). Getting along in a group is like getting along with a friend; a group has a growing personality, too.

If your troop or group is already on target and full of spirit, you can look for ideas on how to keep your good things going and growing. If you hear (or think) that your group "isn't any fun" or "never does anything," you'll find ways to work through tension and toward what you want to do with your group.

"Good Group" Features

Everyone likes the company of others who share the same interests. In the long run, though, what probably matters the most to you is the way in which the members of a group relate to you and to each other. The "good group" features that most people look for depend on the members who:

set an open, friendly tone

act cooperatively, as a team

work in a comfortably sized, personalized way

show a record or potential of success

help the group to be well thought of by others

Together with others in your group, you have the opportunity to use the Girl Scout Promise and Law as you work toward building the friendships and lifelong memories that go with good groups.

When Cadette and Senior Girl Scouts are asked what they value most about Girl Scouting, it's almost always "the people."

Helping and Hindering Roles

As a Girl Scout, you're bound to have the chance to work with different kinds of people who act in different kinds of ways. At some time, certain kinds of behavior show up in every group, for better or for worse. You know: some people are always trying to find ways to agree; others always seem to want their own way.

Any group is helped when someone:

energizes people to do more or do better

harmonizes situations with humor or soothing words

takes care of technical details like windows, handouts, tables, chairs

keeps discussions on target and on time

makes sure no one is feeling left out, no ideas are overlooked

transfers information and inspiration beyond the group

opens the group to other people, new ideas, new opportunities

On the other hand, a group may be hindered when someone:

makes fun of others' values or feelings

interrupts and distracts the group

boasts and shows off, tries to take credit for others' efforts

is never willing to reach out and try new ideas

complains a lot, but never tries to improve things

bosses and bullies people, dominates decision-making

couldn't care less, or says one thing and does another

For a group to balance helping roles and to work through those that hinder isn't always easy. Sometimes, situations can get very tense, tempers can rise. What happens next in your group?

For example, what do you do if people keep interrupting in a meeting? Shushing them or telling them to shut up is a put-down and usually doesn't work for very long. The temporary distraction of getting at the cause of the interruptions is more likely to strengthen your group and save its energy for future efforts. (When you have a headache, rather than just treating the pain, treat the cause of the pain.) Maybe the interrupters are feeling bored or left out, maybe they're bursting with new information or want to try a different idea, or maybe they just need a chance to discuss things among themselves. Until your group does something to spark their interest, pays attention to their input, or considers their ideas, your group has lost part of its team to tension.

Tension — Is It Always a Headache?

The people in your group, on your team, can be a primary resource, but at the same time their actions can be a primary source of tension. How your group uses its energy to face and resolve conflict is a people problem/opportunity.

Looking back at the hindering roles, see how their application in a tense situation would probably make things worse, and the tension would become a negative problem. On the other hand, you can turn conflict into a positive force by using the helpful roles.

Tension can become a negative force in your group if you:

try to run from it, ignore it, hide it

attack and blame people

close your minds to others' views

divide into competing factions

sulk if your side doesn't win

air your differences in public

Tension can spark positive action in your group if you:

see conflict as a signal that something needs changing

confront the situation (not the people) before it gets out of hand

pool your ideas to define the real issues

look for aspects you can agree on

try to find points you like on both sides

think of other ways to look at the situation

involve everyone in compromise so no one loses

Tension arises from such feelings as boredom, ignorance, competition, chaos, or discomfort. But tension doesn't have to mean a headache. Your group efforts can pull you together in a response that's exciting, informed, cooperative, organized, and full of good feelings and fun.

Still, it's not easy to resolve conflict. There's no need to be afraid or embarrassed by it. Your first positive step may be to call for help! But whom can you ask?

People: An Energy Resource for Groups

America's first woman architectural lighting designer Lesley Wheel (center) explains design and technical plans for lighting a new hotel to Senior Girl Scout Darla Jones. Hoosun Wong (right) is an associate designer with the Wheel-Gersztoff office.

Maybe "they" would help! Sometimes, you may hear "they know what to do," or "they help make us feel good."

You must know who "they" are, there's at least one of "them" involved with your group. Right! "They" is a large group of caring adults, one of whom may be your leader, an interest project consultant, or maybe a person whose career appeals to you.

On your way to becoming a woman, growing through girl/adult partnerships is a special part of Girl Scout program. As you work closely with adults to balance your ideas and their ideas, you'll be increasing your capability. You'll get to take on a larger share of responsibility — and the increased freedom that goes along with it. You can even become the adult in partnership with younger girls.

You'll find tips on approaching adult consultants in *Let's Make It Happen!,* pages 8–11. You can use the same ideas to recruit adults for other kinds of girl/adult partnerships, too. In *From Dreams to Reality: Adventures in Careers,* all the activities lead you to think about and then explore your future role as an adult.

Communicating: The Thing to Do

To do anything together, you and the other individuals in a group must communicate first. Whether you just wave or smile at each other, write notes, talk on the telephone, post notices, circulate newsletters, or participate in meetings, the universal thing that groups do is communicate.

As a member of a group, you share ideas, facts, opinions, values, feelings, or needs. Brainstorming and discussion are two special methods groups can use to share ideas.

Brainstorming

Brainstorming is a special kind of communication for collecting a lot of ideas in a few minutes. The key is imagination, not practicality or logic, with everyone spilling out whatever ideas come to mind. When brainstorming:

All ideas are welcome without criticism — that comes later.

The more inventive the idea, the better.

Quantity of ideas is what is needed; quality can come later.

Building on others' ideas is welcome in brainstorming. Select a group recorder, someone who can write fast to keep up with the rush of ideas. Or use a tape recorder. Select someone to start and stop the discussion and agree on a signal to use whenever someone makes a judgmental comment such as "That won't work" or "That's silly."

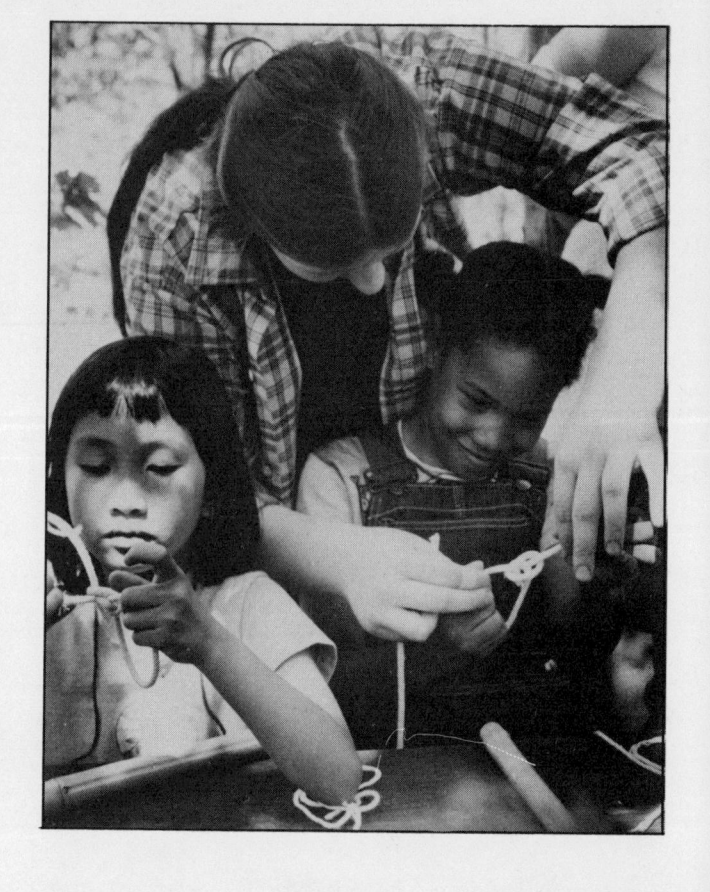

Write the brainstorming subject on a chalkboard or paper that all can see and you're ready to go. The point is to go fast. Each person offers an idea or says, "I pass." Remind yourself that any input counts, no matter how far-out.

When the recorder has collected many ideas, stop and take a look at what you have. Identify: ideas your group can use, ideas that do not seem as if they will work for you, and ideas that might turn into something useful, if developed.

Brainstorming stops when you start judging and choosing ideas to follow through.

Discussion

Group discussion is talking with a purpose. It can help you when you want to exchange ideas, thoughts, and feelings; increase your knowledge about a particular subject; make a decision; or solve a problem. Getting the most out of discussions and using discussion as a step to action takes skill and practice on everyone's part.

Here are some guidelines for leading a discussion:

See that everyone is comfortable. Seat people so that no one feels left out and everyone can see and hear.

Start by stating the purpose of the discussion as simply and clearly as you can.

At first — listen. Let the others talk so you can find out if they know the purpose of the discussion.

Make sure every speaker gets respectful attention. Encourage members who are shy to talk with: "Let's hear what Paula thinks of this"; "Let's be sure we have everyone's ideas."

If things get noisy and confused, raise your hand for quiet. Lowering your own voice to a whisper may get everyone's attention back. Call on people by name to bring them back to the topic. Try to channel enthusiasm and/or spark active listening.

Be prepared with correct information when it is needed or have a resource nearby with the facts.

Learn a few phrases to smooth ruffled feelings, to balance expression of points of view: "You have a good point there, but on the other hand…"; "Mary's right; we do need to consider that. But could we tag it and hold it until a little later?"

Try to get the discussion going back and forth among various members rather than from each member to you.

Summarize the discussion. Repeat the main points that have been made or arguments pro and con and bring an end to the discussion.

If the purpose of discussion is to make a decision or to arrive at a plan or solution, see that this happens.

Voting and Consensus

Voting and consensus are two ways to close discussion with a decision.

Voting can be done by secret ballot, raising hands, standing up, voice, or ballot box. It may be wise to record each vote if the outcome is needed to be pooled with others (patrols to troop, for example; see "Forming a Group" section).

When deciding by consensus, the entire group considers alternatives and tries to come to a decision that all members can support. By considering all points of view, and by combining the best of all alternatives, the group may either reach a consensus (everyone likes the decision), or reach near-consensus (a few members aren't sure but will go along since their ideas were listened to and considered).

Fine Tuning: Continuing Evaluation

Evaluating communications in a group is essential to group success. Eager questions and nodding in agreement are cues to continue.

You will need to observe how well you are holding the attention of the people in the group. Are they eager? Are they making efforts to cooperate? If they are, you can assume they've understood and accepted the group message. If they aren't, you may need to change your approach.

When communication in a group has been open and complete, you know the wonderful feeling of a job well done, the rewards of praise, and the joys of celebrating. Even when there are differences of opinion, the group draws closer if its words and actions have measured up to the Girl Scout Promise and Law. Each individual can feel good about the links of understanding forged with effective communication.

Cadette Girl Scout Erin Williams learns about hair care at Clairol's Consumer Research Center.

Organizing for Action

Getting the who, what, when, why, and how together really requires a group effort. In this section, you will find more about goal-setting, group structures, balancing people and tasks, planning, processes, and record-keeping.

Goal-Setting

Setting goals is the first step toward group action. It's also something you do every day, though you may not always call it that. You need to state, "Here is something I want to make happen." And, for an individual or a group, that's what goals are: statements of something you'd like to see happen or exist in the future. When a group sets goals for itself, it enhances the chances for its own success.

Here are some goal-setting ideas you can use in any group. Put them to work as you head toward group accomplishment.

Make your goal clear — get it in writing...even if it's just on a big piece of paper that everyone can see, agree to, and refer back to as a reminder. Be as specific as you can. (Goals are often stated in terms of "to be _____"; "to be able to _____"; "to complete by _____.") For example:

Our Goal Is: To set up and run an after-school reading clinic at Fairfield Library, beginning by February.

Our Goal Is: To go camping at Clear Lake on the third weekend of January.

Be realistic! Ask yourselves:

Are you really interested enough in this goal to spend your time, energy, and money on it?

Will you have the support you'll need? (parents, Girl Scout council, school consultants?)

What blocks will you need to overcome? Can you? Are you ready to?

If your answers make reaching your goal sound impossible, ask yourselves how you might change your goal or your commitment to it. Being realistic doesn't have to mean putting aside a cherished dream or accepting second-best. Big things are possible, but they'll call for extra effort and imagination.

Mark your path to your goal. Most goals are fairly long-range projections, and you reach them step by step, not all at once. Shorter, in-between steps (usually called "objectives") help you spell out some of the "hows" of reaching your larger goal. For example:

Our Goal Is: To go camping at Clear Lake on the third weekend of January.

Some steps we can take (objectives) are:

Reserve the campsite.

Check the first-aid kit.

Arrange for transportation.

Forming a Group

When forming any sort of group, it is important to keep the group a manageable size and structure. Manageable depends on what you want to do. More than ten can play tug-of-war, but only two can play chess. Formal officers are good sometimes, but not always. Whatever you plan to do, some size and structure will feel especially right for your group. In determining size, consider these things. Discussions can usually handle up to eight or ten participants, but groups where you share very personal feelings might be better if they were smaller. Be ready to break into smaller groups when you feel overloaded. Be willing to join with others when it's to your mutual gain.

Pick the right structure for your group, depending on your purpose — free-wheeling, committee, elected officers. Your group may want to use one of the following group structures, or create another system that combines or is different from any of these.

The **patrol system** has always been special to Girl Scouting. Although Girl Scout labels are unique, the same representative system works well in any group (troop) large enough to divide into subgroups (patrols) that give input to an executive committee (Court of Honor).

The overall troop uses several patrols and a Court of Honor. Each patrol has five to eight members who elect a patrol leader from among themselves. The main purpose of the patrol is to carry on the program in a troop. Because each patrol is small, every member can have a say and a chance to try out leadership roles.

The Court of Honor consists of the adult leader, all patrol leaders, plus a troop treasurer and a troop scribe (secretary) elected from the total group. The Court of Honor acts as a clearinghouse, a coordinating center, and a decision-making body. At its meetings, the patrol leaders voice the ideas and opinions of their patrols, and help to make decisions and plans affecting the total group.

Special assignments for carrying out plans or total-group jobs may be given to the patrols or to task groups specially formed for short-term action. Patrols may make plans and decisions that affect only their own group.

A **steering committee** is a small group within the total group, and is made up of officers and members-at-large elected by everyone. This system can be effective for a large group.

The steering committee gathers ideas from all the members, sorts, plans, and recommends activities. It coordinates activities and events for the total group and involves all members in carrying out plans.

A steering committee sets up and maintains communication within the total group, and between the group and outside groups. An adult leader acts as adviser to the steering committee.

In the **town meeting system,** every member of the group discusses, criticizes, and directly votes or comes to agreement on all total-group business. Subgroups may carry out certain decisions and activities. This system is usually most effective in small groups.

Officers may be elected by the total group to guide discussions and help the group arrive at decisions or members may just take turns carrying out these responsibilities.

Whenever you want to pursue interests or activities that cannot be handled or enjoyed by the total group, a **task group** or subgroup may be formed. Subgroups might be formed to: investigate information on a particular question, plan and/or carry out parts of a total-group project, carry out routine and/or special troop tasks.

Balancing the Load: Delegating Responsibility

Delegating responsibilities is a matter of dividing whatever needs to be done into various jobs, describing responsibilities, and making assignments. It may help to consider job titles for people who will lead (coordinate), direct the action, get things ready, get the job done, clean up, evaluate, carry through on spin-offs.

When delegating responsibility, select people to match jobs. The important thing is to balance the load, making sure that everyone gets an opportunity to cooperate and participate, developing skills as both followers and leaders. Here are a few factors to consider when you look for balance:

overweighting: the same people doing most things

balance between adult leader's responsibilities and those of other members

balance between everyone being "responsible" and specific assignments of jobs. Everyone's job can turn out to be no one's if assignment of specifics is not clear.

Here's another way to look at balance of responsibility in your group. For an agreed-upon length of time (two hours? two weeks? two months?), each member keeps her own log or record of the things she does to aid group action. (She jots down everything she feels are her contributions to decisions, tasks, problem-solving, improving relationships and "go" power of the group.) At the end of the time period, share your logs. You may be in for some surprises.

You can use these sorts of balance checks from time to time while you are planning a project or activity, or when you go back to evaluate progress over a period of time. You can devise similar tools for looking at how responsibilities are shared at home, in school, in various community groups.

Charting Your Course: Planning Ahead

Whether you call it planning, arranging action steps, organizing, or composing, it's like putting together a jigsaw puzzle with pieces of time, activities, resources, and work. Long-range planning involves looking at what you expect to do in the future. Short-range plans only consider what you want to do right away.

How your group works depends on you and your ability to evaluate your progress as you go along. Don't wait for a big failure to discover you should have altered your plan. By paying attention to the details and the little things that happen, you can keep away from problems and pitfalls. Don't be afraid to seek group consensus to change your plans if that seems right to you. Plans are there to help you. You give them a right to exist — and you can change them, too!

Here you'll find even more ways to fill jobs and balance the load. Try different ways at different times according to your needs.

THE SHOPPING LIST

Goal: _____ By: _____
(Date)

List the following:

What needs to be done

By when

How (the how can be decided by the person(s) who will carry out this part of the plan or by the total group)

Who will do it

How much it will cost

Where the money will come from

How often you will check your plan and make changes if needed

THE BIG PICTURE

Chart columns that include:

Activity

Who wants to do it (total group/which members)

How much time it will take

When's the best time(s) to do it or when members can't do it

THE COUNTDOWN

Goal: _____ By: _____
(Date)

Visually work backwards from your target date and fill in each thing that needs doing before then. (You can still make a list of all the things to be done.) Figure out how many days/weeks/weekends you have available to carry out parts of your plan. If all that needs doing won't fit into the time, you may have to change your target date — or work overtime!

THE LONG-RUN CALENDAR

You can use this method when you need to accommodate a number of different activities into a total group action plan.

To get the big picture, use a calendar to identify the activities that will take place during each month. Place an (M) next to those activities that will take place during the regular meeting time and location. Place a (T) next to the activities to be done by the total group. Place an (S) next to the activities that will be done as a subgroup.

Here's a sample of months from a calendar for a group that had many interests.

September
Planning (T, M)
Money-Earning Event (T)
Apply for Wider Opportunities (S)

October
Camping Trip (T)
Auto Mechanics Interest Project (S)
Photography Interest Project (S)

November
Community Action Project (T)
Safe Driving Clinic and Picture Story to combine both interest project group efforts (S)
Auto Mechanics Interest Project (continued)
Photography Interest Project (continued)

December
Holiday Party (International Dinner) (T, M)
Complete Interest Projects (S)

January
Girl Greatness Filmstrip (T, M)
Career Exploration Interest Project (S)
Challenge of Being a Girl Scout (S)
Emergency Preparedness Interest Project (S)

February
Planning and Evaluation (T, M)
Career Exploration Interest Project (continued)
Challenge of Being a Girl Scout (continued)
Emergency Preparedness Interest Project (continued)

March
Council Cookie Sales (T)
Fashion and Beauty Workshop (T)
Community Action Project (S)
Complete Interest Projects (S)

Record-Keeping

Keeping track of everyone and everything in your group can't all depend on memory alone. Records are especially helpful when your group wants to: recall past efforts and evaluations, answer questions about time and money, plan ahead and monitor progress, make agreements and share results, pass on information to new members.

Choosing methods for your group to keep records is an activity in itself! Here are some possibilities: agenda-building, note-taking, budget-building, agreements and accomplishments, roster/attendance/dues, thanks.

Agenda-Building

Be clear about your part in making the agenda (an orderly list of things to be done in a meeting).

Keep notes together, not just in your head or on loose bits of paper.

Organize your notes. Use symbols to alert you to special items. An asterisk might mean decisions to be made, a checkmark could indicate new business to report.

Be sure all facts are complete and correct.

Opinion and decision items should be in question form.

Leave space for notes so outcomes are together, too.

Decide the order of items; keep related ones together.

Set approximate time limits.

Share agenda with members; get their input and agree on timing.

Follow the agenda.

Toward the end, ask for agenda items for the next meeting.

Note-Taking

Taking notes during or shortly after a meeting keeps ideas ready for use as a resource.

Adding details at the time when they're fresh in your mind will make your notes more interesting later. Including names of those involved also adds interest.

Decisions and general agreements should be noted.

Recording the number of votes for and against an issue may be important, too, especially if your votes will be added to others for the final outcome.

Organizing your notes according to the agenda will help keep things in order.

Include how jobs were divided, who was responsible for what, and comments for improvement. Using such notes as a resource helps the next time around. With good notes, your group can avoid "the same old thing" — or keep up with old favorites, whether it's a menu for a cookout or a checklist for an event.

Reporting back, updating absent members, and building the next agenda are all made easier by complete and accurate note-taking.

Budget-Building

Some of what your group does and the plans you make will depend on money. Recording and projecting your needs and the cash required to meet your needs is basically what a budget is all about. Make it a door-opener, not a slammer, in your planning.

Here is a sample work sheet to help you plan a budget for a year. First, figure out your proposed outgo. You might consider the following things.

PROPOSED OUTGO

Girl Scout Annual Membership Dues
(national dues multiplied by number of girls
in the group)   _____

Meeting Equipment
(Do you need things like a new bulletin
board, supplies for the first aid kit?)   _____

Resources
(How much are the records or books you'd
like? *From Dreams to Reality, Let's Make It
Happen!, Planning Trips With Girl Scouts?*)   _____

Continuing Program
(Will you need money for service projects,
activities with your sister troops, or other
long-term plans?)   _____

Flexible Program
(money for spur-of-the-moment ideas)   _____

Highlights
(troop camping, troop trips, councilwide
events)   _____

                                                   _____

                                                   _____

Total Proposed Outgo   _____

Then, figure out a plan to get the group income to match the proposed outgo.

INCOME

Troop Dues
To find out how much each girl might have to pay, divide the total proposed outgo by the number of girls in the troop.

Group Money-Earning Projects
See *Let's Make It Happen!* for ways to go about this. Remember, your group needs written permission from your council before starting a money-earning project. A work sheet will help you explain what the money will be used for.

How much money will you have to balance your troop budget?

From troop dues   _____

From a money-earning project   _____

Agreements and Accomplishments
Keeping track of activities, assignments, and accomplishments will help your group to head off problems as well as add to your bank of resources. Both the interest project agreement in *Let's Make It Happen!* and the guidelines for writing a resume in *From Dreams to Reality* relate to individual spin-offs from a group's experience.

If you write a letter to a consultant, you're making a contact that requires your response, too. See *Let's Make It Happen!* for a sample letter.

Roster/Attendance/Dues
It's a good idea to use the Girl Scout registration form for the basic information. Then add whatever else you may need. Include leaders and consultants, too.

Keep track of dues paid and absences. Include names, dates, and amounts.

Thanks
Thank-you notes and certificates of appreciation come under record-keeping, too. If your group gets them, it's a good idea to keep a scrapbook or display where everyone can share the good feelings. When your group gives them, you might take pictures of the ceremony for your scrapbook or for a news item in your school or community paper. Having everyone sign a certificate adds a personal touch, especially if the signatures become part of a group design.

For Anyone, Anywhere, Anytime

Groups, like individuals, change and grow. One growing experience that is basically the same for anyone, anywhere, anytime, involves taking on a task and working to make it happen. You've been through a basic process to get things done or to solve a problem.

If you ever…	you went through…
designed anything	the creative process
did an experiment	the scientific method
voted	the decision-making process
fixed a leak	the problem-solving process
joined in a service project	the group process

The words you use touch on basic concepts common to artists, scientists, decision-makers, problem-solvers, group members, to anyone

Simplified, the steps in this universal process are:

SENSE: Pay attention to cues all around.

SEEK: Identify resources and gather information.

SORT: Weigh your findings and choose from your ideas.

SHAPE: Transform your ideas into action.

STOP-START: Evaluate and extend your experience and, if need be, go back and start over again.

Usually, the process will flow along in a logical order, following a regular sequence, reaching for a predictable goal. Along the way, you'll cycle and recycle through the steps.

Quickly review a few of the times you've already made this process work for you. Notice that sometimes you may have skipped a step, made a creative leap, moved on a hunch, or gone back to an early stage on the way to your final goal.

There's no reason to feel locked into the exact sequence, or to get bogged down at one stage or another. Just go carefully, aware of the fact that tension, the need to get something done, is the first step and it's up to you to respond. You might pull back or push ahead into any stage of the process.

Use the outlined steps as a guide if your group's in a rut, getting bogged down, or if you don't know where to start or what to do next. Identify your need — a problem to solve, a decision to make, a question to answer, an inspiration to share, a group goal to reach for. Put yourselves on the right track and proceed.

You could call this process "The Wheel of Progress" because it is not a simple chain of steps to a single goal, it is a cycle. Each time you go through the steps, you're ready to start again. Whatever your final outcomes, success or not, you have accomplished something, you have learned something about yourself and the world around you. The next time you start the cycle, it won't be the same because you will have something new to build upon. The final step is a starting step, evaluate and grow.

Each of the five steps in the process can be explained in wider terms.

#

Attention! Start with a need.

Something has to be done.

A choice must be made.

A problem must be solved.

A question has to be answered.

An inspiration should be brought to life.

ALL SENSE

#

Ask yourselves and others for ideas and resources.

Define goals, gather ideas, identify resources.

Identify decision(s) to be made, come up with alternatives.

Collect and analyze information, investigate the situation.

Observe and experiment, gather facts.

Think about ideas, look for possible forms of expression.

ALL SEEK

3.

Make a decision.

Resolve differences.

Consider and predict consequences, evaluate each alternative, make selections.

Suggest and weigh possible solutions. Select for most desirable results.

Interpret information, compare, look for trends and relationships.

Picture an idea, compose an imaginary finished product, shout "Eureka!"

ALL SORT

4.

All together now! Arrange and act.

Construct and implement action steps. Delegate, staff, budget, assign jobs and do them.

Act on the preferred decision. Apply resources toward the desired results.

Try out solution(s) to resolve the problem.

Draw conclusions, establish relationships of cause and effect.

Explain answers.

Transform ideas into something tangible.

ALL SHAPE

#

Evaluate effectiveness, assess needs.

Report on accountabilities. Ask "how much?" and "how well?"

Assess results and actual consequences.

Enjoy relief from the problem.

Explain and extend knowledge.

Display, perform, or publish for others' reactions.

ALL STOP-START

Looking Back, Looking Forward: Assessing and Evaluating

When you've evaluated a success, celebrations are in order so you can really feel good about yourself and your group.

But how do you know when success is yours? And what can you do so that you can look forward to a successful finish? And what if, in spite of all your efforts, you end up disappointed?

A lot of people look at an evaluation as something they do after the action is over. It's good to look back and see what happened and to check results against your goals. But evaluating is more than just a sit-down-and-talk-it-over thing at the end of a project. In planning any group activity or event, evaluating your needs, interests, and expectations and those of your prospective participants beforehand is one of the first guarantees of success.

Then, make the most of the natural tendency to ask yourselves "How's it going?" while it's going. Usually, you can head off disappointment if you're ready to respond to clues from questions that you ask yourselves like:

How well is your plan paying off?

What's the enjoyment level? (Are most people having fun? learning? contributing?)

What seems to be working out well? Where are the snags?

What can you do right now to make things go better or be closer to what you'd hoped for?

How can you focus on improving or salvaging a situation rather than pointing the finger of blame at individuals?

Very, very few activities have results so dismal that the activity can be called a complete failure. Even when a lot of things go wrong, something usually can be salvaged something worthwhile to be learned and applied to make things better. It takes time to accept some mistakes or to see some humor in a "bad" or "dull" activity. But when you do, you can build, even on a bad experience, by picking yourselves up and trying again. Most so-called "failures" are only failures because they are labelled that way. If you can be positive without being unrealistic, you're on the track to useful evaluation and usable results.

Look for:

What have you learned from your "goofs?" How can you avoid them another time or in other situations?

What were your group successes? What helped you toward these? How can you make them happen again?

Are there any individual/personal successes you should recognize? (special efforts? a breakthrough for someone? important contributions of talent, skills, patience, resourcefulness?)

What help do you need to do even more or better? Where or how can you get this help?

In terms of Girl Scout program, during the planning stage as well as afterwards, you can ask yourselves if you've included opportunities for:

acquiring new skills

contributing to society

learning more about yourselves

relating to others

a balance of active and quiet pursuits

a variety of activities in all five worlds of interest or one special interest

exploring your roles and potential as women

interacting with other Girl Scouts

learning about other cultures

fun

You may want to fill-in-the-blanks the next chance you get!

When you evaluate a group activity or event, you measure what you hoped to do, what you did, and how well you did it. Evaluations can help determine the success of your venture, give you clues to improvements for the future, and give you the satisfaction of knowing the job was well done. Think before you ask and think again after you have your answers.

Questionnaires

A questionnaire can be an important assessment tool. It can give you sharp, specific details and is one of the most efficient methods of obtaining evaluations from large numbers of people. If you want an accurate assessment, you need to know what everyone involved thinks. The following are important rules to consider when planning your survey.

Do be specific. Decide exactly what you want to know and ask just that. Avoid general questions.

Don't ask long and involved questions. Keep your sentences short; cover only one point in each question.

Don't use slang or jargon. Words, especially slang terms, can have very different meanings for different people. Don't expect everyone to know what you mean.

Don't ask leading questions. You want an honest answer from the person being interviewed, so make certain your opinion doesn't come out in the question.

Do use a rating scale. Generally, reactions aren't all good or all bad. There are degrees of opinion and providing a rating scale will give you a better idea of the general reaction. A rating scale could look like this:

1	2	3	4	5
good				poor

Do number your questions. Compiling and organizing your results will be easier.

Do keep your questionnaire as short as possible. Stay with the basics. Nobody wants to spend a long time answering questions.

Do narrow down from wide range to more specific items. Follow a logical order.

Do include some opportunity for personal comment by the individuals answering your survey.

Try a "telegram" for evaluation-in-a-nutshell. The next time your group evaluates an activity or project, have each person write an imaginary (or real!) telegram to someone (friend, relative, etc.), giving her thoughts and feelings about the value of the activity. Share your telegrams for group reactions.

Making an evaluation worthwhile involves more than summarizing the results of a questionnaire or keeping notes from an evaluation discussion. Finishing touches like thank-you notes, an awards ceremony, or a celebration party are all ways to recognize a job well done. But they're only part of the finale. Following through on suggestions, keeping in touch with special people, living up to your successes (or rising above your shortcomings) all require continuing attention. Sharing is more than just that telegram to a friend — it's learning from your experience, good or bad. And it's looking forward from a new vantage point, ready to work on your answers to "what's next?"

So, as you can see, the World of People is your world. Why not begin sharpening the skills necessary to be a part of tomorrow by trying the following dabbler interest project? To earn a recognition certificate, do at least eight activities.

TIME FLIES. Look at your community to find signs of change. What are the population patterns? In what ways has your neighborhood changed? stayed the same? Go to a hall of records, historical society, or library, to find out more about the people who settled in your community. Find evidence of their presence in statues, street and business names, architecture, etc. Make a display or produce a pamphlet or newspaper article depicting the things that have changed in your community, as well as those that have not changed, over three or four generations, if possible.

AS THE TWIG IS BENT. Chronicle your heritage by making a family tree. Talk with family members and friends to get all the details. Go back as many generations as you can. Include an explanation of the ways your heritage has affected your lifestyle.

OR

Interview people who are older and compile an oral history and/or pictorial record of their experiences when they were your age. Find out the ways they handled problems similar to and different from your problems.

COME ONE, COME ALL. The world is composed of many ethnic, racial, and religious groups. Make a list of everyone you are in touch with on a daily basis. What groups do these people represent? How did each group come to be a part of your community? Find a way to illustrate your community's diversity — perhaps through a food, craft or book fair, a play, or a poster.

SHOPPING SURVEY. Go to a supermarket, grocery, department store, hardware, or discount store. Make a list of products that are imported. Check with import-export firms or with government (state or federal) commerce offices and find out what things are exported to other countries from your part of the country. Share your findings concerning the interdependence of the peoples of the world.

BRING HOME THE WORLD. Find out about international relations as they relate to Girl Scouts. Learn more about the World Association of Girl Guides and Girl Scouts and participate in a Juliette Low World Friendship project.

NEWSWORTHY. Pick one controversial issue in the news. Read accounts in different newspapers and magazines. Watch television broadcasts and listen to radio coverage. Compare the different points of view. Summarize what you have heard or read in the different sources and present it to a group of people through your local newspaper, church or school bulletin board, or at a community gathering. Ask for reactions to the different points of view. Share your findings.

GET OUT THE VOTE. Participate as a nonpartisan in an election. You might help with voter registration or provide baby-sitting or other services to make it easier for people to vote.

BODY TALK. Look at body language. For one day, observe people to find out the nonverbal messages they communicate. Is it possible to say "yes" verbally and "no" nonverbally at the same time? Talk with friends about the messages you convey. Share your findings with a group of people in church, synagogue, or Girl Scouts.

MEDIA MINDED. Try this activity to help you find out how the media affect politics. Look at media (radio, television, newspaper, magazine) coverages of a political candidate. Listen to or read the verbal message. Try to see the nonverbal message. Think and talk with people about ways a candidate's appearance, tone of voice, or surroundings can affect a voter. Identify ways a candidate is made to look appealing to a voter. Conduct or participate in a campaign for someone in a school election or create a hypothetical campaign strategy for a candidate.

ACTION PLEASE. Survey your community, decide what needs to be done and get busy. With a group or as an individual, participate in a social action project. Although service can be given at a hospital, nursery school, or senior citizens' center, try to find a new way to help people. For example, you might provide child care for a mother who needs some time to be away from her family, or you might help in a neighborhood renovation project, or in making a camp or park more accessible to the disabled. (See the "Reader's Digest Foundation Grants" section for a possible funding source.)

THE INSIDE STORY. Look inside yourself for stereotyped ideas you might have about people. Analyze them. Were they based on personal experiences or the experiences of other people? Weigh your emotional knowledge against your intellectual knowledge to find if your feelings have a basis in fact. Look at illustrations in magazines and newspapers for evidences of stereotypes held by others. Create a picture, write a story, or collect news articles to illustrate ways stereotypes can be eliminated.

WITH JUSTICE FOR ALL. Investigate your legal rights and responsibilities as they relate to civil issues. How old must you be to drive, vote, marry, enter into a contract agreement for credit, or to start a business?

OR

Find out your rights as they relate to criminal justice. Talk with a lawyer about the rights of juveniles and how they differ from the rights of adults. Find a way to educate young people about the law. You might make posters, write a news article, or conduct a law education clinic or mock trial.

Where Do You Go from Here?

Did you enjoy your exploration in the World of People? How about learning some more? For example, why not start a cultural sharing project within your community? Maybe you could help persons new to this country to learn about it and to become citizens. Teach Brownies about how the diversity in this country and in the world can lead to greater understanding among all people. Look around; you will find many exciting ways to learn about people, and you just might learn more about yourself, too.

Resources

Consultants: local Board of Elections, business people, Chamber of Commerce, historical societies, League of Women Voters, legal aid and human rights organizations, libraries, psychology teacher, social worker.

National Organizations: get in touch with your local chapter first, or write to the national address given here.

American Civil Liberties Union
Juvenile Rights Project
22 East 40th Street
New York, N.Y. 10016

Anti-Defamation League
B'nai B'rith
823 United Nations Plaza
New York, N.Y. 10017

The Juliette Low World Friendship Fund
Girl Scouts of the U.S.A.
830 Third Avenue
New York, N.Y. 10022

Learning and Media Research
Southwest Educational Development Laboratory
211 East Seventh
Austin, Tex. 78701

National Conference of Christians and Jews
43 West 57th Street
New York, N.Y. 10019

National Trust for Historic Preservation
1785 Massachusetts Avenue, N.W.
Washington, D.C. 20006

T.V. Action Center
c/o National P.T.A.
700 N. Rush Street
Chicago, Ill. 60611

U.S. Census Bureau
Washington, D.C. 20006

World Association of Girl Guides and Girl Scouts
The World Bureau
132 Ebury Street
London, S.W. 1, England

Books

Fersh, Seymour (ed.) *Learning About Peoples and Cultures.* Evanston, Ill.: McDougal, Littell & Co., 1974.

Gersten, Irene, and Bliss, Betsy. *Ecidujerp-Prejudice: Either Way It Doesn't Make Sense.* New York: Franklin Watts, 1974.

Sussman, Alan. *The Rights of Young People.* New York: Avon Books, 1977.

Get Ready for the World of Today and Tomorrow

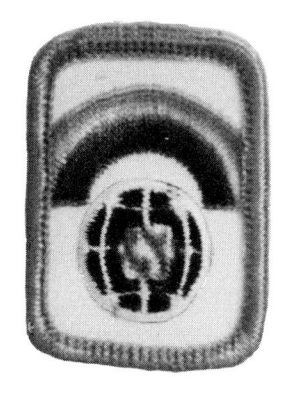

What can you be sure of in the World of Today and Tomorrow? One thing, definitely, you can be sure of change. Whether it's a new business practice, the latest discovery in the natural or physical sciences, a new tool to revolutionize industry, or a just-discovered way to harness energy, the latest news will be old news tomorrow. Creative minds are changing the world around you in everything from cooking to communication. Your energy and imagination are needed in these times when the scientific wonder quickly becomes commonplace. The possibilities are endless and can open new horizons as rapidly as today's laser travels to tomorrow's space station. Your ideas may be the ones needed to open up a whole new and better life for everyone.

If you're ready to spend today looking into an exciting future for yourself and others, then this dabbler interest project is for you. Doing eight or more activities will earn you a recognition certificate.

WATERWORKS. Follow the path pollutant oil takes into the waterways. Because most oil pollution in America's waters comes from vehicle engines and not from major oil spills, use discarded car motor oil in a simulation. (You might use the oil obtained when doing "Oil Those Gears," on page 12 in *Let's Make It Happen!.*) First you fill a large glass jar with layers of sand, then gravel, fine stones, soil, and crumbled plant material. Then spread the oil over the top of your "ground." Periodically, "rain" on your "ground" by sprinkling the jar with water. Record what you see happening to the oil after one week, six weeks, longer. Try varying the combinations of layers. How does oil reach streams, rivers, lakes, oceans?

OR

Find out how jetties, breakwaters, bulkheads, or dams affect the flow of water and the materials it moves. Make drawings or take photographs to show how these structures have directed the flow of water, sand, and other materials.

CREATURE FEATURE. Try your skill at being an animal trainer. A family pet may be ready for a new trick or perhaps you can start with a different animal, such as an insect, frog, or fish. Make absolutely certain you know the food and home needs of your animal. Decide carefully what you will teach and how you will reward. Find out about your animal and be reasonable in what you expect. Always treat your animal in a kind and humane manner. Some ideas to start with could be having your animal run a maze, respond to a signal, find a hidden object, or perform a new maneuver. For one month, keep a record of your training progress. Compare this exercise with your own learning experience: any similarities? differences?

WHETHER WEATHER. Can you be a weather forecaster? What does that weather map in the newspaper or on television really mean? Find out the meaning of the symbols used on the map, how high and low pressure areas, direction and speed of winds, temperature and land features affect your weather. Track at least two storms as they form and move across a part of the earth. From what you see happening with these storms, predict what will happen in your area as other storm systems start. Check your forecast with the actual weather.

OR

Collect or make your own weather instruments. Keep a record of the weather for several weeks and compare your readings with the official ones in your area. Find out about the very sophisticated equipment a meteorologist would have.

IT ALL ADDS UP. Design, plan, and construct something you or someone else can use. Once you know what you want to build, your important first step will be to do a rough outline of your basic design. Do try to experiment with various shapes and sizes. Use the sketch to do a scale drawing of your design.

Whether it is a storage chest, dog house, horse stall, platform bed, or whatever item you need, make certain you have precise measurements because this plan will determine the type and quantity of the materials you'll use. You should know the length, width, height, and area dimensions to determine the amount of building materials, such as wood, paint, glue, nails, etc., that are required. Investigate different kinds of material as alternatives, for example, plywood versus wooden boards, or stain instead of paint.

You should know your options, so shop around then compare prices. Use your imagination; a clever idea can substitute a less costly item for an expensive one. Decide when quality justifies the expense. Your final choice will depend on the amount of material you'll need, the overall design, and your budget. Build your piece. Keep track of all your plans and figures so you can compare your finished product with your original plan.

OR

Become an expert at scoring a team sport, such as bowling or softball, so you can keep important statistics for the team, such as individual and team batting averages. Act as a scorekeeper for a school team, recreation commission team, or church or synagogue league.

SPREAD THE WORD. Long ago a town crier walked through a town and shouted the news. Today there are many ways to tell people what is happening in the world. Visit a newspaper printing office, telephone company, radio or television station, or a school business office near your home and find out how information is collected and shared. What equipment are they using? How has their equipment changed during your lifetime? Find out what changes are now being made in the way this facility communicates. Design a futuristic way to spread the word to your friends or someone far away. Share your design with others through words and drawings.

DO IT YOURSELF. Be able to maintain and do safe simple repairs on one or more of the following:

  bicycle, car (change tire, lubricate)

  faucet (change washers)

  lamp/electrical plug (rewire)

  power lawnmower (change oil, clean and set the gap on the sparkplug)

  sewing machine (clean and lubricate)

  window (recaulk, replace broken pane of glass)

OR

Try one or more of these do-it-yourself ideas: Assemble a piece of technological equipment, such as a radio or telescope, with a kit or your own materials. Design and construct a model of a bridge or building structure. Learn how to operate a home or small business/school computer.

NIGHTWATCH. Plan and carry out an expedition, overnight if possible, to explore the night sky. If you make certain you have a clear night, you should be able to see many different things. Observe as many of the following as possible: a planet, meteor, your zodiac constellation, stars of different colors, an artificial satellite, the North Star. Plan ahead and try to be out on a night during a special celestial event, such as a lunar eclipse, meteor shower, comet appearance, or special planet grouping. Take a telescope or binoculars to aid in viewing. Make a record of your exploration.

BIG BUSINESS. With a group, create a marketable product using the individual skills of each person. You might make food, clothing, a household item, holiday decorations, or gifts. Keep track of the money needed for your raw materials. Use advertising techniques to market your product in your community. Sell your product or make it part of a money-earning event. Assess the satisfactions, frustrations, and important needs associated with running a business: investment, productivity, marketing, and profit-making.

FLY A KITE! Assemble or build your own. Experiment with your kite to find out how to control it and which winds are best. Modify your design to make it fly better. Enter a kite-flying contest or festival, or organize one of your own in your community. Find out about kite flying or kite fighting in a country other than the United States.

TRY SOME MAGIC. Put on a chemical magic show to entertain a group of people. Look up some interesting and colorful experiments in a "how to" book on magic. Try to find at least three tricks that involve a bit of chemical magic. Be sure you can explain "what's happening" to the audience.

TIME PAST. Conduct an archaeological investigation. Archaeology is the scientific study of the remains of historic or prehistoric peoples and their cultures. It includes examining their living areas, tools, clothing, writing, and other remains. Try to find an archaeological site to investigate. Visit a prehistoric site to collect information or see if you can join a "dig." If this is not possible, visit an area of historical significance, such as a house, factory, or town square constructed at the turn of the century or earlier. Obtain important information by checking county courthouse records and by interviewing older people familiar with the area. Take photos and record interesting features about the site. You might like to write a short story about one day in the life of a past inhabitant of your site, or re-create a past skill or craft, such as dyeing, tool making, or a recreational pastime.

FOODSTUFF. Grow an improved seed. Through genetic research and technology, most cultivated fruits and vegetables are now superior to those grown 50 years ago. Get some new hybrid and/or disease-resistant seeds and cultivate a "superplant." If you don't have garden space, grow your plant in a large container. Scan a seed catalog and find out what other varieties of your plant can be grown. Share your findings and your crop with your troop, friends, or family.

OR

One concern today is to make certain there is enough nutritious food for all the people in the world. Find out as many different ways to get nutritious food as you can. Select at least one way and see how the process for getting, preparing, or preserving and/or taking this food to market has changed in the past ten years. Some food sources to consider are raising pigs, chickens, or cattle; growing grain or fruit; or harvesting fish, seaweed, or other food from the water. Share this information with your group or another interested group.

Where Do You Go from Here?

The topics covered in this section are only a starting point in opening the World of Today and Tomorrow. The worlds of science, math, technology, and business are unlimited in their possibilities for tomorrow and you have sampled only a small fragment of what they offer today. If these activities have stirred your interest and you would like to explore further, consider writing your own interest project. Develop a project in one of the fields you enjoyed or in a new one that was not even touched upon. (See *Let's Make It Happen!*, page 69.) *Girl Scout Badges and Signs* can also provide you with a wide range of ideas. And don't forget your consultants, they can offer a great deal. The World of Today and Tomorrow is knowledge, creativity, energy, and a look to the future. Take your place in it.

Resources

Consultants: college sports information director, garden club members; math, chemistry, science, or shop teacher; pet shop personnel; planetarium director.

Local Groups: business persons' organization, county cooperative extension service, environmental or ecology group, garden center, town historical society, area weather bureau.

National Organizations: get in touch with your local chapter first, or write to the national address given here.

American Society for the Prevention of Cruelty to Animals
Education Department
441 East 91st Street
New York, N.Y. 10028

National Association for Girls and Women in Sports
1900 Association Drive
Reston, Va. 22091

National Oceanic and Atmospheric Administration
Public Affairs
11400 Rockville Pike
Rockville, Md. 20852

U.S. Coast Guard, G-WEP-4/TP 12
Washington, D.C. 20593

U.S. Department of Agriculture
Publications Division
Office of Government and Public Affairs
Washington, D.C. 20250

U.S. Environmental Protection Agency
Office of Press Services
Washington, D.C. 20460

Girl Scout Resources
Exploring the Hand Arts. Cat. No. 19–994, (rev. ed.) 1977.
Toolcraft. Cat. No. 26–214, 1976.

Books
Bascom, Willard. *Waves and Beaches: The Dynamics of the Ocean Surface.* (rev. ed.) Garden City, N.Y.: Doubleday & Co., 1980.

Cobb, Vicki. *Magic…Naturally: Science Entertainments and Amusements.* New York: J. B. Lippincott, Co., 1976.

Growing Vegetables in Containers 564H, *Growing Your Own Vegetables* 565H, *Simple Home Repairs, Inside* 158H. Available from the Consumer Information Center, Pueblo, Colo. 81009.

Percy, John R. *Observer's Handbook* (Astronomy). Buffalo, N.Y.: University of Toronto Press.

Porter, Sylvia. *Sylvia Porter's Money Book: How to Earn It, Spend It, Save It, Invest It, Borrow It, and Use It to Better Your Life.* Garden City, N.Y.: Doubleday & Co., 1975.

Rush, Anna Fisher. *McCall's How to Cope with Household Disasters.* New York: Random House, 1976.

Thomas, Bill. *The Complete World of Kites.* New York: J. B. Lippincott, Co., 1977.

Yolen, Will. *The Complete Book of Kites and Kite Flying.* New York: Simon & Schuster, 1976.

Creativity Is the Key to the World of the Arts

Art is all around you, it isn't just an "old master" tucked away in a museum. It's something everyone can enjoy and make part of her/his daily life.

Art is the visual arts you appreciate with your eyes: the paintings, drawings, collages, prints, photographs you see in homes, public buildings, books and magazines and, yes, in museums, too.

Art is sculpture and buildings, the plan of a city, the pottery and furniture you use, and all the arts you can appreciate for the beauty of their form and their practical use as well.

Art is the performing arts of music, dance, drama, and puppetry that you can see live or appreciate on recordings, film, or television.

Art is everyday practical things, the design on the package you buy, the poster you see, flower arrangements, the colors and patterns in rooms, the way you dress, the way a park is landscaped.

The World of the Arts in Cadette and Senior Girl Scouting can be the introduction to lifelong pursuits. Some people may find they wish to make a career of one form of the arts. But even if you do not pursue art as a career, it can be a hobby or avocation and bring you many hours of lasting joy.

Try this dabbler interest project first and then go on to the interest projects in *Let's Make It Happen!*. Do eight activities to earn a recognition certificate.

CREATIVITY IS THE KEY. "Creativity is the capacity to see new relationships and possibilities in familiar objects or situations." Using this definition, create from your imagination and materials readily available to you a game for others in your troop or group to play. Make up all the rules and parts or equipment for the game. Have a game-sharing session and decide which were the most creative games.

MASTER BUILDER. Architecture is an art form you live with every day. You work and play, eat and sleep in architecture. You see it constantly and it affects your life more than you realize.

Design and create a model out of styrofoam, cardboard, or wood that you feel would be a dwelling for a city or farm approximately ten years from now. Be able to explain the basis of your design and how it relates to the lifestyle you project.

VISUALIZE. Paintings, prints, and textiles are three forms of the visual arts. To get started, do one of the following: create an original painting in acrylic, oil, watercolor, gouache, or mixed media that expresses something about you and your life. Your painting can be a portrait, a landscape, abstract, or realistic.

OR

Create an original print (relief print, serigraph, lithograph, etching, or mixed media) that can be used as a poster, page for a calendar, or a greeting card.

OR

Create an original design for embroidery. Transfer the design to fabric for a pillow or wall hanging or to an article of clothing. Embroider your design.

THE THIRD DIMENSION. Three-dimensional arts are those you can see from all sides, such as sculpture, mobiles, pottery, furniture, and some textiles. Choose a spot in your home, school, town, public building, or park that you feel might be enhanced by a work of three-dimensional art. Create the three-dimensional design full-scale or, if your choice is a large sculpture, make a small scale model.

MUSIC HATH CHARMS. The music that particularly appeals to you may be the popular songs of today, Gregorian chants, opera, chamber music, atonal electronic, jazz, folk, rock, spirituals, or baroque. For this activity, choose a musical form that combines with other arts: an opera, operetta, or musical. Listen to one of these on the radio or a recording or watch one live, on television, or in a movie. Then create a fun-time activity booklet or a puppet show that will help someone else learn about that particular work. Make suggestions for instrumental and vocal music in your activity book.

OR

Put on a performance that explains a musical form for a group. Include music, both instrumental (or recordings) and vocal.

"THE WORLD'S A STAGE." There is more to theater arts than just acting. To find out about one aspect of the theater, explore the role of the mask. Why are the sad and happy masks used as a symbol of the theater? Look at the drama masks of the American Indian, ancient Greeks, African or Asian masks. Put on a dramatic reading or a short playlet using masks. Be involved in making a mask of papier-mâché or other material and in staging or reading in the production.

ON YOUR TOES. Dance is a natural form of expression. Whether it's the exuberance of the current popular dance or the square dance, the quiet beauty of the ballet, or the exotic drama of the dance of faraway countries, it can be participated in and appreciated by almost everyone. Here's a way to begin learning how to share dancing with others. Participate in a square or folk dance. Write down, draw, and/or record the music so that you will be able to teach someone else. Now find a group to teach and get your students dancing, too.

OR

Plan a dance (of any type) in which some parts are danced by a group and some parts by individuals. Ask some friends to join you. Try out movements, decide whether your dance tells a story or is a plan in space. Then perform the dance and find some method to write it down so others can do it.

THE MIND'S EYE. The camera can be an artistic medium as well as the means of recording events and places. Photographs can tell a story, or be hung on a wall to enjoy as one would enjoy a painting. Create a photographic story on a theme of your choosing. Use one roll of film, or at least eight photos, to tell your story.

OR

Create a slide/tape presentation or a film that is intended to teach or present an idea to an audience. Your presentation should run at least two minutes.

JUST FOLKS. In almost every country and every period of time, art forms have been created by people without formal art training. These are often called folk arts. They include woodcarving, basketry, pottery, weaving, spinning, quilting, embroidery, furniture-making. Start exploring the riches of folk art by finding examples or pictures and descriptions of five different kinds of baskets or pottery, either from other countries or from the United States. Choose one type of basket or pot and make a small sample basket or pot in the same method. Explain to others why you chose the one you did, and what materials you used and why.

MIRROR, MIRROR ON THE WALL. Look at yourself in a full-length mirror. Think about what would look best on you. Is it stripes or plaids? going up and down or around? What color would be good? deep purple, brown, light pink? What about the fabric texture? heavy nubby wool or smooth draping polyester? all one color or a separate look? After you have made these decisions, design an outfit that reflects what you think would be best for you.

IT'S YOUR PLACE. Interior design and residential architecture are to homes what fashion design is to a body. You use the same principles of color, line, proportion, texture, and harmony to create a pleasing and livable environment. To get a feeling about what is involved, do one or both of these activities.

Imagine you have only one room in which you must live, work, and entertain. You haven't much money to furnish it. Draw a plan for the room, including furniture you would buy or make. Indicate the other aspects of the room: window coverings, fabrics, colors, floor coverings, and storage space.

OR

Plan your dream apartment or house by making a scale drawing of the interior on graph paper. Indicate doors, windows, closets, electrical outlets, and other standard items the way an architect would.

COMMUNICATION IS THE GAME. Every day you see around you ways in which art communicates a message. Create a poster promoting or advertising an artistic event, or design a package for Girl Scout cookies. In either case, use lettering and some other form of visuals for your design: illustration, photographs, etc.

OR

Write a message. Write a poem, short story, speech, or article that conveys the meaning, importance, or worth of the best book you have ever read.

Where Do You Go from Here?

If you have enjoyed the activities in the World of the Arts and wish to continue, there are many things you can do. Special courses or workshops offered in your community can give you further help in a subject you especially enjoy, such as a photography course or workshop at an art museum. If you are interested in an art project not in *Let's Make It Happen!*, you might be able to get together with a group of girls to work on (for example) dramatics. Get in touch with a local little theater group and perhaps write your own interest project on the subject. (See *Let's Make It Happen!*, page 69.) You can also find many helpful suggestions in *Girl Scout Badges and Signs*.

Resources

Local Groups: art museums, art schools, camera clubs, dance groups, department stores, dress shops, ethnic and cultural clubs, music groups, theater groups.

Girl Scout Resources

Exploring the Hand Arts. Cat. No. 19–994, (rev. ed.) 1977.

Sing Together: A Girl Scout Songbook. Cat. No. 20–206, 1973.

Skip to My Lou. Cat. No. 20–199, 1958.

Books

Andrews, Wayne. *Architecture in America.* (rev. ed.) New York: Atheneum Publishers, 1977.

Berger, Melvin. *The World of Dance.* New York: S. G. Phillips, 1978.

Bradley, Duane. *Design It, Sew It, and Wear It.* New York: Thomas Y. Crowell Co., 1979.

Chieffo, Clifford T. *Silk-Screen As a Fine Art.* New York: Van Nostrand Reinhold Co., 1979.

Corrigan, Barbara. *Of Course You Can Sew.* Garden City, N.Y.: Doubleday & Co., 1971.

Gascoigne, Bamber. *World Theatre.* Boston: Little, Brown & Co., 1968.

Haskell, Arnold. *The Wonderful World of Dance.* Garden City, N.Y.: Garden City Books, 1960.

Hautzig, Esther. *Redecorating Your Room for Practically Nothing.* New York: Thomas Y. Crowell Co., 1967.

Horn, George F. *Visual Communication: Bulletin Boards – Exhibits – Visual Aids.* Worcester, Mass.: Davis Publications, 1973.

Kodak Publications: Available from Eastman Kodak Company, Dept. 841 GS, Rochester, N.Y. 14650.

Mills, John Fitzmaurice. *Painting for Pleasure.* New York: Galahad Books, 1977.

More, Janet G. *The Many Ways of Seeing: An Introduction to the Pleasures of Art.* Cleveland: William Collins Publishers, 1969.

Paine, Roberta M. *Looking at Sculpture.* New York: Lothrop, Lee & Shepard Co., 1968.

Pettit, Florence H. *How to Make Whirligigs and Whimmy Diddles and Other American Folkcraft Objects.* New York: Thomas Y. Crowell Co., 1972.

Price, Christine. *Made in West Africa.* New York: E. P. Dutton, 1975.

Scheffer, Victor B. *The Seeing Eye.* New York: Charles Scribner's Sons, 1971.

Slade, Richard. *Modeling in Clay, Plaster, Papier-Mache.* New York: Lothrop, Lee & Shepard Co., 1968.

Sullivan, George. *Understanding Architecture.* New York: Frederick Warne & Co., 1971.

Wachsberg, Joseph. *The Story of Music for Young People.* New York: Pantheon Books, 1968.

Weiss, Harvey. *Lens and Shutter.* Reading, Mass.: Addison-Wesley Publishing Co., 1971.

———. *Paint, Brush and Palette.* Reading, Mass.: Addison-Wesley Publishing Co., 1966.

Znamierowski, Nell. *Weaving, Step by Step.* New York: Western Publishing Co., 1967.

Periodicals

Art & Man, published six times yearly. Subscriptions available from Scholastic Magazines, Inc., 50 West 44th Street, New York, N.Y. 10036.

Come into the World of the Out-of-Doors

What is it that:

molds and unites a group, and provides time to laugh together?

mobilizes your muscles to paddle, pull, push, hike, hold on?

challenges your abilities to think clearly, to plan for a safe journey?

tempts you to see where a path, stream, or wave goes, or where the current will take you?

uses the skills of a whole group—navigator, humorist, planner, leader, songster, and follower?

challenges you to be observant and wonder why a lichen survives on a harsh rock surface, but not in polluted air; how a tall tree anchors itself in shallow soil?

lures you to the top of a hill in the predawn chill to watch the sunrise?

It is the World of the Out-of-Doors. This world provides you with all these opportunities and more.

The challenge of the outdoors has always been a high point of the Girl Scout experience. There are four interest projects in *Let's Make It Happen!* which can help you learn more about "Camping," "Eco-Action," "Outdoor Survival," and "Wildlife" and lead to outdoor adventures.

By doing at least eight activities in this dabbler interest project, you will be sampling the unlimited possibilities in the World of the Out-of-Doors, and earn the interest project certificate.

WATER — IT'S LIFE ITSELF. Design a puppet show, an interpretive trail for a day camp, a wide game for a troop, a film story, or a canoe trail to tell others why clean water is vital for life. Use local examples to show all the things that water does: how plants and wildlife use it and conserve it; the sources of water, how and where it flows, and what it carries with it; the difference between a wetland and a watershed; how nature purifies and removes wastes from water. Don't forget to portray its beauty, changing shapes, sizes, and colors.

WINTER WONDERLAND. Winter's snow and cold sometimes inhibit people's planning for outdoor activities. But winter is a time when woods, fields, and hills take on a special beauty in their white coats. Plan a winter hike, overnight, snowshoe or skiing trip to take a special look. Discover for yourself how snow and other natural forces change the shape of the landscape. Look for the tracks of animals that climb, that hop, that have hooves. Look for the gnawings of porcupine, beaver, deer, rabbits. Find out how the winter inhabitants tap into the high energy food sources in seeds and nuts. Enjoy the silhouettes of trees, rocks, clouds, weeds, and seeds. Find a way to share your discoveries with others.

ROUTES TO THE PAST. Trace a part of the trail or course that American Indians, explorers, settlers, or merchants used to reach your community. See if you can find evidence of the modes of transportation which they used. Figure out the relationship between the local geography and the way people and goods moved through the area. Design a way to share this part of your community history with others.

ON WHEELS. Explore a nearby community, follow a bike trail, chart your own route for a biking adventure, or lay out a bike route for others to follow. Whichever cycling adventure you choose, know how to take care of yourself and your equipment, be familiar with bicycle regulations in your community and your state.

HORSEBACK RIDING. There is a thrill in learning to communicate with your horse, whether it is in a ring, on a trail ride, or a pack trip. Western, Hunt, or English? It's up to you. Get in touch with groups in your community who own, or have access to, horses and are knowledgeable about them. Ask the group to help you develop or perfect your riding skills. Take part in a trail ride, plan a series of short rides on trails or bridle paths, participate in a horse show, or attend an exhibition of Western or show riding.

LET'S EAT. Become a whiz at preparing tasty meals for yourself and your group to suit the different outdoor adventures you have planned. For example, plan a high energy, no-cook meal to eat along the ski trail, or a gourmet meal served in style at your campsite. Plan and prepare three or more different meals in the open to complete this activity. Use a portable stove for at least one of these meals.

BACKPACKING. A good way to see the unspoiled beauty of the natural world is to backpack. Prepare a plan to update your camping and safety skills, and physical endurance. Carry out your plan, culminating in a backpacking trip.

OR

Prepare an exhibit, based on your experiences, showing the personal and group equipment, and the supplies needed by a party of eight for a weekend backpack trip. Indicate changes (if any) for a week-long trip. Share this information with a group of less experienced backpackers.

ORIENTEERING. Here's an organized sport that uses a compass and map to get participants from one place to another in the shortest time possible. Orienteering is also an outdoor survival skill, which anyone going away from traveled highways should master. Test your ability with compass and map on familiar ground before you start bushwhacking through unfamiliar territory. Invite a consultant to help your group become proficient in the use of a compass and in map reading, or use some of the following "Resources" to develop a game to interest others in the art of orienteering.

MAP IT/MAKE IT. On a map of your area, locate navigable rivers, lakes, ponds, and other waterways. Indicate small craft landings, campsites, and canoe liveries. Navigate at least one of these waterways, keeping a log of the trip to share with others.

OR

Select or make a canoe paddle appropriate for your use. Design a personal symbol for it to identify it as yours. Add other symbols to the paddle blade or shaft to record your participation in canoe trips, canoe meets, or games.

WATERWAYS. Figure out ways to make it easier and faster to move a canoe, rowboat, or sailboat through the water. Try feathering your oars or paddle, sculling with a single oar, or trimming your sails. Show that you can propel your craft if the main propulsion fails, if you lose an oar or paddle, or if the wind dies.

SENSE ALERT. While on an outdoor trip, take time to look at and enjoy natural textures, colors, symmetry, silhouettes, and shadows. Learn to use a magnifying glass, binoculars, or a telescope to add new dimensions to your world. Keep a log of the things you learn about your environment by seeing, hearing, smelling, and feeling. You may discover ways to:

read cloud patterns to forecast the weather,

tell the prevailing wind direction by the shape of the plants,

tell about the activities of wildlife from food or tracks left behind,

tell the difference between the sounds birds make as notes of alarm and those for defending nesting territories.

TAKE CARE! Camp maintenance is a year-round job. Who is responsible for the jobs that must be done to keep your Girl Scout campsite or a nearby park in good condition? Do you know what you, as a user, can do to care for the equipment and site you use? Talk to the person in charge of maintenance, or check for yourself the many kinds of jobs to be done or the special skills needed to do the work. Find out what kind of jobs you or your group can do or learn how to do. Agree upon a time to do a "contracted" job of volunteer site service or take part in a scheduled workday or work camp to maintain the site.

OR

Vandalism is defined as the willful or malicious destruction or defacement of property. Often it is a simple and thoughtless act, such as carving initials on a picnic table or misusing a campsite. Find something at camp or in your community that has been vandalized, such as a tent marked with graffiti, a defaced bus stop, or destroyed vegetation. Decide how long it took to vandalize this and why you think it was done. Then estimate the cost and the amount of time it will take to have the damage repaired, replaced, or removed. If possible, help with the repairs or develop a way to prevent future vandalism.

Where Do You Go from Here?

If you have enjoyed doing the activities in the World of the Out-of-Doors and wish to continue, there are many things you can do. For example, if your group would like to try an extended bicycling trip, find a consultant who can help you develop a plan to learn the skills you need to know. The consultants could also help you write your own interest project on bicycling. (See *Let's Make It Happen!*, page 69.) You can also find helpful suggestions in *Girl Scout Badges and Signs.*

Resources

Local Groups: camp horsemanship association; hiking club; local, state, and national parks; Sierra Club chapter.

National Organizations: get in touch with your local chapter first, or write to the national address given here.

American Horse Council
Suite 300
1700 K Street, N.W.
Washington, D.C. 20006

National Safety Council
Bike Safety Division
444 N. Michigan Avenue
Chicago, Ill. 60611

U.S. Department of the Interior
Heritage, Conservation and Recreation Service
Washington, D.C. 20240

U.S. Geological Survey
Public Inquiries Office, Room 1036
General Services Building
19th and F Streets, N.W.
Washington, D.C. 20244
(Free map catalog, request by state.)

U.S. Orienteering Federation
Box 1039
Ballwin, Mo. 63011
(Information on local clubs and orienteering meets.)

Girl Scout Resources

Be an EQ Traveler. Cat. No. 19–966, 1971.

I Am a River. AV 13–78, 1971.
(This is a 35 mm color filmstrip, with script for narration, 15 minutes long.)

Books

Alexander, Taylor R., and Fichter, George S. *Ecology.* New York: Western Publishing Co., 1973.

American Red Cross. *Canoeing.* (rev. ed.) Garden City, N.Y.: Doubleday & Co., 1977.

Amos, William H. *The Life of the Pond.* New York: McGraw-Hill Book Co., 1967.

————. *The Life of the Seashore.* New York: McGraw-Hill Book Co., 1966.

Basic Canoeing and Kayaking, Basic Outboard Boating, Basic Rowing, Basic Sailing. Available from your local American Red Cross chapter.

Bennett, Joseph W. *Vandals Wild.* Portland, Oreg.: Metropolitan Press, 1969.

Bike Basics, A Guide to Bicycles, Bicycling and Safety. Available from American Automobile Association, Traffic and Engineering and Safety Department, 8111 Gatehouse Road, Falls Church, Va. 22042.

Browder, Sue. *American Biking Atlas and Touring Guide.* New York: Workman Publishing Co., 1974.

Bunnelle, Hasse. *Food for Knapsackers and Other Trail Travelers.* San Francisco: Sierra Club Books, 1971.

Kauffman, Sandra, *Kauffman's Manual of Riding Safety.* New York: Crown Publishers, 1979.

Kjellstrom, Bjorn. *Be Expert with Map and Compass.* New York: Charles Scribner's Sons, 1976.

Look, Dennis A. *Joy of Backpacking.* Sacramento: Jalmar Press, 1976.

Mitchell, Jim, and Fear, Gene. *Fundamentals of Outdoor Enjoyment.* Tacoma, Wash.: Survival Education Association, 1976.

Neiring, William A. *The Life of the Marsh.* New York: McGraw-Hill Book Co., 1966.

Price, Steven D., et al. *The Whole Horse Catalog.* New York: Simon & Schuster, 1977.

Reader's Digest. *Joy of Nature.* New York: W. W. Norton & Co., 1977.

Teaching Orienteering by J.W. Gilchrest. Available from Orienteering Services, P.O. Box 347, LaPorte, Ind. 46350.

Tejada-Flores, Lito. *Wildwater: The Sierra Club Guide to Kayaking and Whitewater Boating.* San Francisco: Sierra Club Books, 1978.

Thomas, Dian. *Roughing It Easy.* New York: Warner Books, 1976.

————. *Roughing It Easy, 2.* New York: Warner Books, 1978.

Usinger, Robert L. *The Life of Rivers and Streams.* New York: McGraw-Hill Book Co., 1967.

Van Matre, Steve. *Acclimatization.* Martinsville, Ind.: American Camping Association, 1972.

The Highest Awards in Girl Scouting

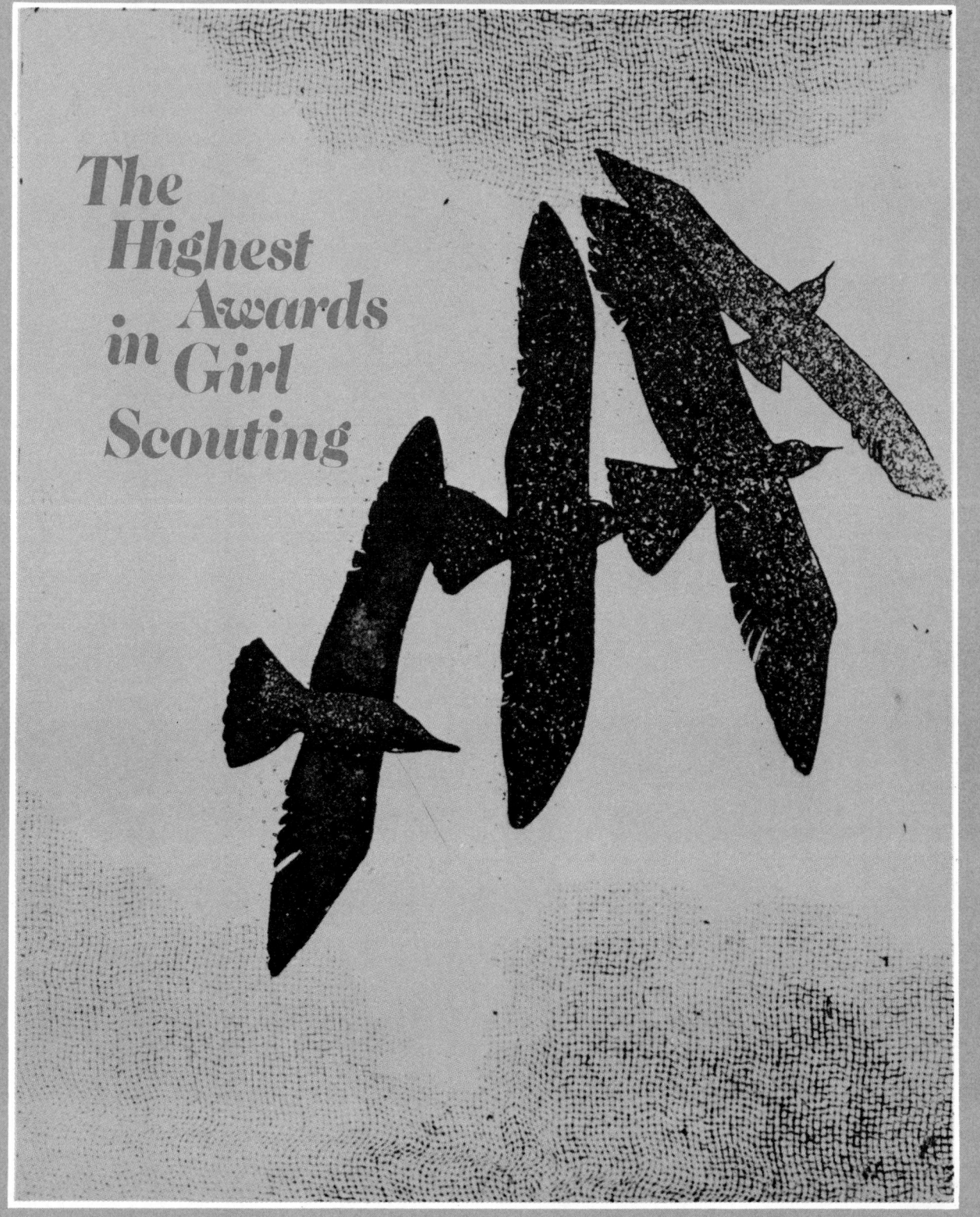

Print, Miho Koshido, age 14, Roselle, Ill.

If you are ready to bring together living by your values, developing new skills, planning for your future, serving your community, taking the lead to meet present and future challenges — in your Girl Scout program and in your life — you are ready for special recognition.

The Girl Scout Silver Award is designed for Cadette Girl Scouts, but may be earned by Senior Girl Scouts. The Girl Scout Gold Award is designed for Senior Girl Scouts.

To earn one of the Girl Scout highest awards requires hard work and a willingness to take on significant responsibility. Your efforts express a special commitment to yourself, your community, your world, and the future. You will need determination and endurance to carry out these special programs. The path to each award requires choices, decision-making, and the ability to follow a plan you have set for yourself that is neither short nor easy. But, with conviction and a commitment to work, in close partnership with your leader, you can succeed.

The Girl Scout Silver Award

You may begin working on this award when you become a Cadette Girl Scout. You may do these four requirements in any order you choose.

1. Earn the Challenge of Being a Girl Scout.

2. Earn three interest project certificates.
(**Note:** It is possible to substitute one tan badge earned as a Junior Girl Scout or as a Cadette Girl Scout for one of the interest project certificates, as long as it did not count toward earning a Junior sign.)

3. Earn the Career Exploration interest project certificate. (See *Let's Make It Happen!,* page 15.)

   OR

   Earn the From Dreams to Reality activity certificate. (See *From Dreams to Reality: Adventures in Careers,* page 8.)

4. Earn the Silver Leadership Award.

The Girl Scout Gold Award

This award is the highest achievement in Girl Scouting. Before you begin to meet the requirements for it, you must meet one of two prerequisites.

Prerequisites

Earn the Girl Scout Silver Award.

OR

Do the following:

1. Complete the Challenge of Being a Girl Scout.
2. Complete five activities, each from a different interest project. Each project must represent a different world of interest. Then do seven or more additional activities to earn a certificate in one of these interest projects.
3. Complete four activities from the Career Exploration interest project.

   Or

   Complete the following activities from *From Dreams to Reality: Adventures in Careers:* two Insights, two Closeups, and two Tryouts.
4. Earn the certificate for the Leadership interest project.

   Or

   Earn the Silver Leadership Award

Requirements

You must be at least 14 years of age or a Senior Girl Scout before making your Initial Application for this award. (See requirement 5A.)

You may do the first four requirements in any order you choose. Of these, no more than one requirement earned prior to age 14 or Senior Girl Scout membership may be applied toward the earning of the award.

1. Complete the Challenge of Living the Promise and Law.

2. Earn four interest project certificates.

3. Earn the From Dreams to Reality Pilots certificate.

   OR

   Carry out a paid or unpaid work experience (of at least 25 hours). Share your understanding and newly acquired skills with others. Document your experience in a log. Evaluate it with your group or through writing a resume. (See *From Dreams to Reality: Adventures in Careers,* pages 28–29.)

4. Earn the Gold Leadership Award.

5A. Complete the Initial Application for the Girl Scout Gold Award and send it to your Girl Scout council office for approval at least eight months in advance of the date you plan to complete these requirements.

   AND

5B. Submit the Final Application for the Girl Scout Gold Award to your Girl Scout council office at least eight weeks in advance of your completion date.

(**Note:** If you complete an activity or interest project or fulfill a time commitment to satisfy one requirement of an award, you may not count that same effort a second time to meet another requirement of that award or of any other award. However, in the case of time commitments, with the agreement of your leader you may increase your time commitment to satisfy two requirements. For example, if you take training and work 25 hours as a hospital volunteer to earn a volunteer service bar, you might work 25 *more* hours as part of your work on requirement 3 of the Girl Scout Gold Award.)

Program:
Design Your Own

What do you do when the things you want to do can't be found in Girl Scout program materials? The answer to this question is easier than you might guess: you design a program of your own.

You might choose to put your activities in an interest project format, such as an Our Own Troop's or Our Own Council's interest project. If you choose this way, see *Let's Make It Happen!,* page 69, for additional guidelines on writing interest projects.

Maybe your activities would slip into a Challenge, or qualify for a volunteer service bar or leadership award. If so, decide on a reasonable way to do this with your group. Agree on your plan before you start doing the activities, especially if earning a recognition is involved. In every case, your Program Planning Agreement can be used, perhaps with modifications, to record your plan in brief. You will probably need to develop additional materials to get all the specifics down on paper.

Designing a program of your own essentially encompasses five steps: deciding on a goal, identifying resources, planning activity stages, doing activities, and following up. You might find it helpful to use a chart with these headings for your own program.

1. Deciding on a goal

The first step in planning your program is to decide exactly what you want to get out of your effort. What do you want to learn about? What do you want to have done by the time you are through? What new skill do you want to have? What level of skill do you want to reach? What is *your* goal?

Here are some examples of goal statements:

"I want to learn to program a computer to do my algebra problems."

"Now that we're in our teens, we feel we can handle more freedom and make more decisions on our own. But our parents are nervous, and sometimes we don't handle things very well when we do have the freedom. We get pressure from our friends and it's hard not to go along with the crowd. We want to get along better with others and, at the same time, do what we have decided is best for ourselves. Could we get a project consultant who is a human relations professional—someone like a psychologist or clergyperson—to help us develop these skills?"

"We want to train to run in our city marathon next year."

"I want to learn techniques for working with the deaf. Then I can be a program volunteer in a Junior Girl Scout troop composed of girls who are deaf."

2. Identifying resources

After you have decided what you want to do, identify the resources, people, and things, that you will need.

In Girl Scouting, your first resource is your leader. She/he is there to be your partner in planning to offer advice and help in moving things along.

Your council is an equally valuable resource: staff or neighborhood volunteers can help you in many ways if they know what you have in mind right from the start. They could: provide information on local resources available to you, such as consultants and printed materials, and help you get in touch; share what other Girl Scout groups have done in your interest area; and share advice related to program standards, health and safety guidelines, and security guidelines.

After you have explored the resources available through Girl Scouting, you may wish to look in your community for other people, places, and things. Can your family members advise you or join as consultants to your group? What organizations might have members who can help you? Can teachers, health officials, or government officials guide you? What books, magazines, newspapers, movies, and television/radio programs could give you ideas and information? Does a public or private facility—museum, business, school—have things you could share or borrow, such as tools, a meeting space, gym, or workshop?

3. Planning activity stages

Be realistic about the time your chosen activities will take. Consider the total hours and the total length of time. For a longer project, you can shorten your path by dividing your plan into phases. Each phase then forms a shorter program that can stand on its own. Or, you can move along, one phase at a time, with something wholly different (a trip? camping weekend?) to refresh your group in between phases. By making your time and energy commitment reasonable, you will make your project more enjoyable.

Your consultants may be able to help you with allotting time to your best advantage. Often consultants know best all the smaller steps you will need to take to get where you are going.

4. Doing the activities

You will want to do your activities in a way that invites maximum interest and participation. Try to balance your activities as much as possible by choosing activities that call for different levels of energy, some active, some less active; by choosing activities that use all of your abilities: thinking, reading, moving, talking, working with your hands, writing, researching, evaluating; by doing some activities in a large group, some in a smaller group, others on your own. Try not to over-use one resource if others are available.

5. Following up

Effective follow-up of an exciting activity often begins even before the program starts. If you want to see yourself on the evening news, you need to plan for television coverage of your Girl Scout event way in advance. Not everything you do will be so new or different as to be newsworthy in the eyes of a producer or editor, but some things may be.

Learn how your council works with the media so you can provide the kinds and quality of information needed for effective public relations. If you have kept complete records, you will have the details to share with your council. In addition to promoting Girl Scouting to the community, you can use these records to tell other members about what you did.

Finally, your records will help you evaluate the success of your program. As your group looks back, with the specifics in front of them, you will find ways you might have improved your plan. By recognizing the weak spots in last week's plan, you can be sure of a better experience next time around.

Planning an Event

Planning an event could be called the challenge of "how to think of everything." The details of planning can seem endless, but if you organize in advance, many of your tasks will be simplified. Try to be as thorough as possible and predict your needs, but be prepared to add or subtract items as you go along.

As an individual, you might assume responsibility for almost all of the planning for a small event for members of your own group. Usually, representatives from several troops or groups are appointed to serve on the planning group, when an event involves a large number of troops or Girl Scouts from other councils. In either case, your leader or consultant appointed by your council will be available to assist when you need advice.

In the book *Safety-Wise* (GSUSA, Cat. No. 26–205, 1977) the "Checkpoints for Specific Activities," "Girl Scout Program Standards," and "Girl Scout Camping Standards" will help you to think of the many things you need to consider in planning an event. In addition, you will find that the steps for planning and problem-solving found in the "Organizing for Action" chapter of this book helpful. Some of the checkpoints you will want to consider as you develop your plans are:

The Preliminaries

- ☐ the purpose of the event
- ☐ theme/focus
- ☐ desired result

- ☐ desirable number of participants
- ☐ qualifications and requirements

- ☐ who is in charge
- ☐ what everyone's responsibilities will be
- ☐ what other groups can get involved

Program/Site/Equipment/Materials

- ☐ type of program needed: camping event, conference, service project, workshop

- ☐ advance preparations and setup
- ☐ scheduling
- ☐ breaks for meals, snacks, or relief time
- ☐ comfort of participants
- ☐ moderators, directors, consultants, guest speakers
- ☐ written confirmation of all essentials

- ☐ selection of time and date/rain date
- ☐ accessibility of site location
- ☐ estimated travel and check-in time needed
- ☐ transportation available, public and/or private
- ☐ parking facilities

- ☐ living/program facilities available
- ☐ reservations, permits
- ☐ safety requirements
- ☐ rest rooms

- ☐ chairs, tables, podiums
- ☐ audiovisual equipment
- ☐ electrical outlets, adapters, extension cords
- ☐ display materials
- ☐ specific items participants will need
- ☐ backup equipment

- ☐ eating areas/cooking facilities
- ☐ restaurants, catering
- ☐ dietary restrictions of participants

- ☐ overnight accommodations: hotels, camping areas
- ☐ reservations, fees
- ☐ provision for showers, bedding, linens
- ☐ home hospitality possibilities

Safety and Security
- ☐ necessary security plans and procedures
- ☐ emergency plans, procedures, numbers
- ☐ first aid available
- ☐ fire precautions
- ☐ see *Safety-Wise*

Public Relations and Promotion
- ☐ announcements and/or invitations
- ☐ posters and flyers, newspaper/media announcements
- ☐ press releases, photographs
- ☐ registration forms, programs
- ☐ welcoming committee or person
- ☐ preparations for speakers, guests
- ☐ thank-you notes

Budget
- ☐ investigate sources of money: present assets, money-earning, participant fees, donations, discounts
- ☐ itemize costs
- ☐ get written estimates or contracts
- ☐ decide how to pay bills: cash, checks, purchase orders
- ☐ what will be done with profits, if any
- ☐ what will be done about losses, if any
- ☐ refunds or cancellations

After the Event
- ☐ return materials
- ☐ replace damaged materials
- ☐ evaluation
- ☐ recommendations for the future

Ceremonies: Special to Girl Scouting

Ceremonies are some of the most important events in Girl Scouting, and often some of the most memorable. You can plan a ceremony in much the same way you would an event, but keep the following in mind:

Make the ceremony honor the personality and the accomplishments of any special participants.

Bring people in who can add something special.

Make the purpose of Girl Scouting, living the Promise and Law, an important part of the ceremony.

Include the council, its work and its role, when appropriate.

Balance the joy and the solemnity of the event.

Practice a ceremony in advance. In order to be effective, ceremonies need to run perfectly, without a hitch. Try to make everything close to what it will be during the ceremony: use the actual props, music, and room arrangement. Don't forget to rehearse introductions, speeches, and presentations.

Occasionally, guests may be invited to your ceremony. They might be family members, troop committee members, another troop, consultants, or members of a sponsoring group. Some ceremonies lose their meaning if they become a "show" for an audience. For ceremonies in which you make or renew your Girl Scout Promise, or express deep feelings and hopes, indicate the highly personal nature of this to your guests in advance. If they will also be participating, be prepared to give them directions at the appropriate time.

Investiture, bridging, rededication, Girl Scouts' Own, Court of Awards, candlelight, and flag are ceremonies that are particularly significant to you and to other Girl Scouts. The Girl Scout Silver Award and the Girl Scout Gold Award may serve as themes for developing a troop's own special ceremony.

Investiture

An investiture ceremony is held when you or others join Girl Scouting for the first time. If you join for the first time as a Senior or Cadette, you will make the Girl Scout Promise and receive the Girl Scout membership pin when you are invested into Girl Scouting. Because there is no set rule on when to receive the World Association pin, this too might be included in the investiture ceremony.

Bridging

This is a ceremony to send you on to the next Girl Scout level and troop. In a bridging ceremony you are received into the new troop with your old troop in attendance. It might include a symbolic bridge and a ceremonial crossing of the bridge. Your favorite songs, poems, or readings composed by you or by your troop may mark this passage.

When you and other Cadettes and Seniors are working with younger Girl Scout level troops or carrying out inter-troop events, you will need to have skills for planning with others as well as the ability to demonstrate and to serve as good examples.

Rededication

You may wish to have a rededication ceremony, separate from a bridging ceremony, at some time during the troop year. This is a time to renew your Promise and review what the Girl Scout Law means to you. It is a time to remember your personal beliefs, values, and commitment. A candlelight ceremony or Girl Scouts' Own is often part of a rededication ceremony.

Girl Scouts' Own

Planned by you and other Girl Scouts, a Girl Scouts' Own can take place anytime, anywhere. Its main purpose is to create an atmosphere of thoughtfulness, sharing, and aspiration toward all the Girl Scout ideals.

A Girl Scouts' Own may be a carefully planned and rehearsed ceremony created by a small group and participated in by your entire group of Girl Scouts. Or it may be an almost spontaneous moment when you and all the members of the troop reflect together on some shared experience.

A Girl Scouts' Own has a theme or central idea, such as the beauties of nature, courage, friendship, messages of music, creation of a better world, and so on. You may express this theme in many ways: through a story, poetry, quotations, or your own words; through music and song; by the spontaneous sharing of thoughts; or through drama.

Court of Awards

This ceremony to present Girl Scout recognitions can be held several times during the year, or as often as your troop wants to plan for it. Your leader can help arrange those parts of the content that reflect recognition and pride in your accomplishments. In particular, when you or a sister Girl Scout are receiving the Girl Scout Gold or Girl Scout Silver Award, the ceremony should demonstrate Girl Scouting's pride in this achievement.

The Court of Awards is a celebration of excellence, which will be a treasured memory in years to come.

Summary of Girl Scout Recognitions

The Girl Scout recognitions and awards system offers something unique at each Girl Scout level. If you choose, you can continue to wear recognitions and awards earned at a previous Girl Scout level.

Recognitions and awards include:

For Brownie Girl Scouts: Brownie B patches, one Dabbler badge, Bridge to Juniors, and Brownie Wings.

For Junior Girl Scouts: Badges (green and tan), Junior Aide patch, Sign of the Rainbow, Sign of the Sun, Sign of the Satellite, and Bridge to Cadettes.

For Cadette Girl Scouts: Badges (tan), the Challenge of Being a Girl Scout,* the Silver Leadership Award,* and the Girl Scout Silver Award.*

For Cadette and Senior Girl Scouts: Interest project patches and certificates; From Dreams to Reality activity patch, Pilots pin, and certificates; and volunteer service bars and certificates in Girl Scouting and in each of the five worlds of interest.

For Senior Girl Scouts: The Challenge of Living the Promise and Law,* the Gold Leadership Award,* the Ten-Year Award, and the Girl Scout Gold Award.

*Note: The Challenges, Leadership Awards, and Girl Scout Silver Award are listed under the Girl Scout age level for which they were designed, but any of them may be earned both by Cadette and Senior Girl Scouts.

Girl Scout Glossary

Baden-Powell, Lord and Lady. Robert Baden-Powell was the founder of the Boy Scout and Girl Guide movement for boys and girls. Olave, his wife, was the World Chief Guide. He rhymed "Baden" with "maiden" and "Powell" with "Noel." Also called "B.P." and "Lady B.P."

Badge (proficiency). An embroidered, cloth symbol earned by Junior Girl Scouts to indicate increased knowledge and skill in a particular subject. Background colors are green or tan. Cadettes may earn the latter.

Bridging. The move from one program age level of Girl Scouting to the next, e.g., from Cadette to Senior Girl Scouting.

Brownie Girl Scout. A Girl Scout who is 6 through 8 years old or in the first, second, or third grade.

Buddy System. A safety practice in which girls of equal ability are paired to help and to keep track of each other.

Cadette Girl Scout. A Girl Scout who is 12 through 14 years old or in the seventh, eighth, or ninth grade.

Camp Counselor. A staff member at a Girl Scout camp.

Campus Girl Scout. A Girl Scout who is 18 through 21 years old who belongs to a Campus Girl Scout group while attending college, or working in a college community.

Candlelight Ceremony. An optional ceremony where candles are used for symbolic purposes. For example, three large and ten small candles may be lit to represent the parts of the Promise and Law.

Color Guard. The Girl Scouts who carry, guard, raise, and/or lower the flag or present the colors at a meeting or ceremony.

Consultant. An adult whose knowledge and experience can aid Girl Scouts in the completion of an interest project or other Girl Scout activity.

Council, Girl Scout. A corporation, chartered by Girl Scouts of the U.S.A., responsible for the development, management, and maintenance of Girl Scouting in a defined area (jurisdiction).

Council, National. The membership body of the corporation, Girl Scouts of the U.S.A., in meeting assembled. Membership consists of delegates elected by Girl Scout councils, the members of the National Board of Directors and the National Nominating Committee, and other persons elected by the National Council when assembled.

Court of Awards. A ceremony that can be held any time during the year at which badges, recognitions, and awards are presented.

Court of Honor. One form of governing body for a Girl Scout troop. Members of the court include: the patrol leaders, the troop scribe, the treasurer, and the troop leader(s).

Daisy. An official Girl Scout magazine for girls 6 through 11 years old, published by Girl Scouts of the U.S.A.

Daisy. The nickname of Juliette Gordon Low.

Eco-Action. The Girl Scout term for learning about the environment and taking care of it.

Event. A wide scale activity for Girl Scouts planned by a troop, council, or group of councils.

Executive Director. The chief executive officer in a Girl Scout council.

Friendship Circle. A symbolic gesture in which Girl Scouts form a circle by clasping each others' hands. It is often used as a closing ceremony.

From Dreams to Reality. A career program for Cadette and Senior Girl Scouts, one part of a three-part program for these age levels.

Girl Guide. The original name for Girl Scouts, still used currently in many countries.

Girl Scout Birthday. March 12th is the Girl Scout birthday, because it marks the first meeting of Girl Scouts in the U.S.A. in Savannah, Georgia, in 1912.

Girl Scout Group. A temporary or permanent assembly of Girl Scouts, who do not use the traditional troop form of organization.

Girl Scout Handshake. A formal way of greeting other Girl Scouts by shaking the left hands while giving the Girl Scout sign with the right.

Girl Scout Insignia. All pins, patches, badges, or other recognitions worn on the Girl Scout uniform.

Girl Scout Leader. A national Girl Scout magazine sent to all registered adult members, and to Senior Girl Scouts who want to subscribe.

Girl Scout Sign. The official Girl Scout greeting. The right hand is raised shoulder high with the three middle fingers extended and the thumb crossing over the palm to hold down the little finger.

Girl Scouts' Own. A quiet inspirational ceremony that has a theme and is planned by Girl Scouts and their leader.

Girl Scout Week. An annual celebration during the week of March 12th, the Girl Scout birthday.

Interest Project Patch. An embroidered cloth symbol earned by Cadette and Senior Girl Scouts to indicate increased knowledge and skill in a particular subject.

International Post Box. A service that provides pen pals for Girl Scouts and Girl Guides. A pen pal can be obtained by writing to the International Post Box at national headquarters.

Investiture. A special ceremony in which a new member makes her Girl Scout Promise and receives her membership pin.

Junior Girl Scout. A Girl Scout who is 9 through 11 years old or in the fourth, fifth, or sixth grade.

Kaper Chart. A chart that shows the delegation of jobs and rotation of responsibility day by day and/or meal by meal.

Leader. An adult volunteer who meets regularly with a troop/group of Girl Scouts in town or camp.

Let's Make It Happen!. A book of interest projects and activities for Cadette and Senior Girl Scouts, one part of a three-part program for these age levels.

Motto. "Be prepared."

National Equipment Service (NES). The national staff department that sells uniforms, insignia, accessories, camping equipment, and printed materials used in Girl Scout program. Local NES agencies are located in licensed stores and some Girl Scout councils.

Neighborhood Chairman (or service unit director). The adult volunteer chairman or head of a service team. The service team is responsible for organizing and delivering service to Girl Scout troops in a geographic subdivision within a council. Also called a service unit.

New Games. A style of noncompetitive, safe, fair, fun, and interesting play that encourages total group participation.

Our Own Troop's Interest Project. An interest project developed and designed by a group with a special interest, following the guidelines in *Let's Make It Happen!,* page 69.

Patrol. A group of girls, no larger than eight, that is a subgroup of a Girl Scout troop.

Pilots. A first-hand work experience as outlined in *From Dreams to Reality: Adventures in Careers,* pages 55–60.

Program Emphases. Four interrelated areas of focus in Girl Scout program, defining what Girl Scouting strives to offer each girl. They are: deepening her awareness of self as a unique person of worth; relating to others with increasing skill, maturity, and satisfaction; developing values to give meaning and direction to her life; contributing to the betterment of her society through use of her own talents and in cooperative effort with others.

Quiet Sign. The Girl Scout signal for silence in a group situation. The person in charge raises her/his right hand and the Girl Scouts present fall silent and raise their right hands.

Ranger. (1) A member of the maintenance staff at a Girl Scout camp. (2) The term for the oldest age grouping in many Girl Scout and Girl Guide associations in other countries.

Recognition. An acknowledgement of accomplishments in Girl Scout program. It may be a pin, certificate, patch, badge, or letter.

Rededication. A formal ceremony at which a girl who was previously invested renews her Promise.

Safety-Wise. A Girl Scout publication for adults who work with girls. It outlines safety principles and supplies safety references for specific Girl Scout activities in the form of program and camping standards.

Scribe. The troop secretary.

Senior Girl Scout. A Girl Scout who is 15 through 17 years old or in the ninth, tenth, eleventh, or twelfth grade.

Service Team. A group of adult volunteer workers who provide direct service to troops within a neighborhood or local geographic unit.

Slogan. "Do a good turn daily."

Town Meeting. A system of government in which the total group makes the decision.

Trefoil. The international symbol of Girl Scouting. The three leaves of the trefoil represent the three parts of the Promise.

Troop. The basic unit in Girl Scouting consisting of the girls, an adult leader(s), and sometimes troop committee members.

Wide Game. A game, with a special theme, that combines a contest, sporting event, and treasure hunt.

Wider Opportunity. Any Girl Scout activity that takes girls outside their own troops and councils.

World Association Pin. A pin with a gold trefoil on a blue field that may be worn by all Girl Scouts and Girl Guides. It is a symbol of the worldwide bond of Girl Scouting and Girl Guiding.

Wyoming Trek. A wider opportunity for organized groups of girls who travel as self-sustaining units to Girl Scout National Center West in Wyoming.

Page References for Answers to Quizzes on Page 12

Girl Scout Quiz

1. Page A-2
2. Page A-5, The Girl Scout Organization
3. Page A-6
4. Page A-11, The World Association
5. They all can. For even more ideas, see pages A-4 and A-5, Your Place in Girl Scouting.

Group Quiz

In this quiz, there is often more than one right answer. The following page references will lead you to think out answers that are right and best for you and your group.
1. Page A-21, People: An Energy Resource for Groups
2. Pages A-24 and A-25, Forming a Group
3. Page A-20, Helping and Hindering
4. Page A-32
5. Pages A-28 and A-29, For Anyone, Anywhere, Anytime

Index

**Special thanks are due to the following for their
contributions and encouraging support:** the girls
and leaders as well as the numerous council volunteer and staff members, national volunteers and staff
who contributed ideas and critical review of the con-
tent; and authors/contributors Anita L. Alcantara, Ruth
R. Boyd, Patricia Connally, Lucy Dinnes, Cindy Ford,
Mary M. Gilmore, Carol N. Green, Mabel A. Ham-
mersmith, Sharon Woods Hussey, Carolyn L. Kennedy,
Verna Lewis, Edith C. Loe, Lynn Ann London, Joan
McEniry, Elizabeth Munz, Corinne M. Murphy, Alicia I.
Pagano, Charlotte Parker, Nancy H. Richardson,
Roxanne Spillett, Valerie M. Tennent, Jo Ann
Wesnitzer.

Program 7/80, 11/80, 10/81